Thomas Cook and Son

Cook's Centennial Programmes

Showing how to Get to America, where and how to Live at Philadephia...

Thomas Cook and Son

Cook's Centennial Programmes

Showing how to Get to America, where and how to Live at Philadephia...

ISBN/EAN: 9783744791748

Printed in Europe, USA, Canada, Australia, Japan

Cover: Foto ©Andreas Hilbeck / pixelio.de

More available books at **www.hansebooks.com**

COOK'S
Centennial Programmes,

SHOWING

HOW TO GET TO AMERICA; WHERE AND HOW TO LIVE AT
PHILADELPHIA; WHERE TO GO AND HOW TO TRAVEL
IN THE UNITED STATES AND CANADA;

NOTES OF

THROUGH TICKETS

FROM

AMERICA

FOR

ORDINARY TRAVEL AND CIRCULAR TOURS TO ALL
PARTS OF EUROPE AND ROUND THE WORLD.

WITH A

NEW COLOURED MAP

OF

ATLANTIC STEAMSHIP ROUTES,

AND A

TOURIST MAP OF CENTRAL EUROPE.

THOMAS COOK & SON,
LUDGATE CIRCUS, AND 445, WEST STRAND, LONDON;

COOK, SON & JENKINS,
WORLD'S TICKET AND INQUIRY OFFICE, CENTENNIAL EXHIBITION
GROUNDS, PHILADELPHIA; 261, BROADWAY, NEW YORK;
And at Boston, Washington, New Orleans, Pittsburg, San
Francisco, and Philadelphia City.

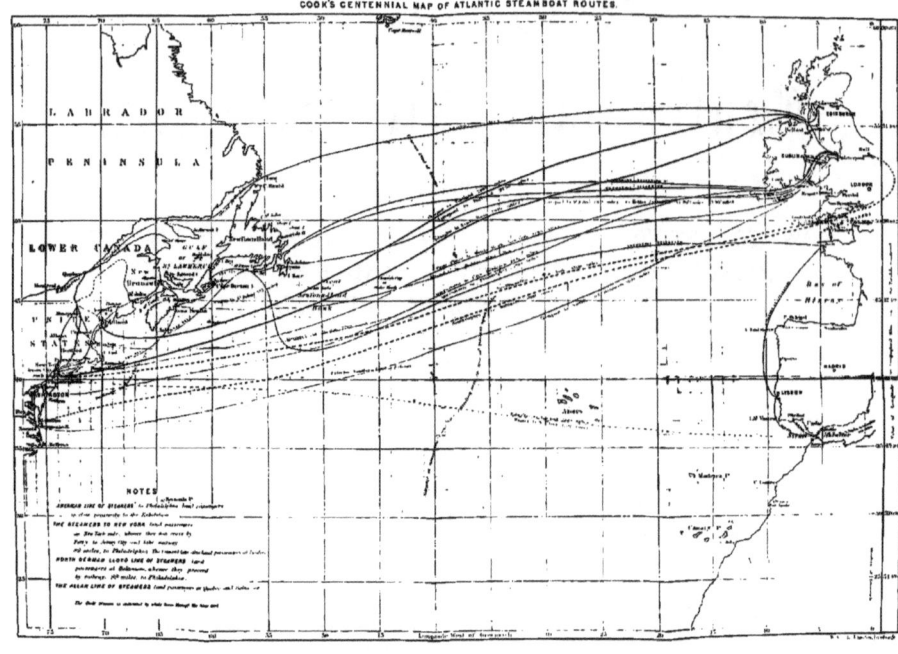

CONTENTS.

	PAGE
MAP OF ATLANTIC STEAMSHIP ROUTES.	
TOURIST MAP OF CENTRAL EUROPE.	
Appointment as General Passenger Agents by the Royal British Commission	5
Steamboat Bookings	8
Through Fares from Continental Cities	9

STEAMBOAT LINES FROM LIVERPOOL, WITH FARES AND SAILINGS:—

Allan Line	10, 11
American Line	12, 13
Cunard Line	14, 15
Inman Line	16
White Star Line	17
Dominion Line	18
Mississippi Line	18

FROM BRISTOL—

Great Western Line	19

FROM GLASGOW—

Anchor Line	20, 21
State Line	22

FROM HULL AND SOUTHAMPTON—

Wilson Line to New York; also to Sweden and Norway	23, 24

FROM HAMBURG AND SOUTHAMPTON—

Hamburg American Line	25

Steerage Rates	25
Our Railway Connections	26
Accommodation for Visitors to Philadelphia	27
Hotels in America, China, Japan, and India	28
Lodging-house Agency	28
Where to go in America	29
Model Programmes and Itineraries	31 to 34
Personally-conducted Tour from France and Belgium	35 to 40
Tours from Scandinavia to the Centennial Exhibition	41 to 44

	PAGE
Models of Tours, starting from Philadelphia—	
First Division—To Chicago, Niagara Falls, Montreal, White Mountains, Boston, &c.	45, 46
Second Division—To Denver, Colorado, Silver Mines, Rocky Mountains, &c.	47
Third Division—To Salt Lake, Yosemite Valley, California, &c.	48
Tour from Scotland	49
Personal Companionship and Assistance	49
Tour Round the World	49
TOURS FROM AMERICA TO EUROPE AND THE EAST	50
Ireland and Scotland	50
England and Wales	51
France	52
Switzerland	52
Italy	53
Belgium, Holland, and the Rhine District	53
Germany, Bavaria, and Austria	53
Scandinavia	54
Spain	54
The Nile and Palestine	54
Mediterranean, Arabian, Indian, Chinese, Japanese, and Pacific Steamship Tickets	55
Personally-conducted Tours	55
List of European and Eastern Hotels	56 to 59
List of Offices and Agencies of Thos. Cook & Son	60
Cook's Tourist Arrangements	62, 63
Midland Railway—Pullman Cars	61

CENTENNIAL EXHIBITION.

APPOINTMENT BY THE ROYAL BRITISH COMMISSION,

AND

CONCESSIONS OF THE GENERAL COMMISSION OF THE CENTENNIAL EXHIBITION.

THOMAS COOK & SON, more than a year ago, received from the Executive of the British Commission of the Philadelphia Exhibition of 1876 a voluntary communication, of which the following are the principal paragraphs :—

THE INTERNATIONAL EXHIBITION OF 1876, PHILADELPHIA.

Offices of the British Executive,
5, Craig's Court, Charing Cross, S.W.
GENTLEMEN,— London, 4th March, 1875.
His Grace the Duke of Richmond, K.G., Lord President of the Council, bearing in mind the able manner in which you conducted the transit arrangements to and from Vienna, both to the satisfaction of the Royal Commission of which his Grace was a member, and to the advantage of the British Exhibitors and visitors to Vienna, has instructed me to offer you the appointment of General Passenger Agents for the British Section of the International Exhibition at Philadelphia in 1876.

His Grace, aware how well the arrangements you effected at Vienna worked for the interests of all concerned, desires that similar, and, if possible, greater, facilities may be afforded in Philadelphia, viz. :—That your special representative on this, as on the occasion alluded to, should be under the immediate orders of the British Executive, and that upon any complaint made to it or its representative at Philadelphia against any member of your staff, and the same being found justified by the facts, your Superintendent shall be bound to follow the instructions and obey the orders of the British Executive.

In naming you "General Passenger Agents for the British Section," His Grace wishes you to understand, and to convey distinctly to all concerned, that the British Executive does not in any way hold itself responsible for delay, loss of luggage, or for any other similar claim. Following the Vienna precedent, it is also to be distinctly understood that suitable offices are to be provided at Philadelphia, to which will be attached a sufficient staff conversant with the usages of the country, and competent to give reliable information to British visitors of all classes. These arrangements to last during the whole period of the Exhibition.

I shall be glad to receive your reply to this letter with as little delay as possible.

I have the honour to be, gentlemen, your obedient servant,
P. CUNLIFFE OWEN,
To Messrs. THOMAS COOK & SON, *Executive Commissioner.*
Ludgate Circus, Fleet Street, London.

Gratefully appreciating the honour of this appointment, THOS. COOK & SON have done their utmost to promote the interests and convenience of British exhibitors, and to facilitate the laudable efforts of the Royal

British Commission in reference to the transport of articles for exhibition and the steamboat passages of exhibitors and their workpeople. It has been their pleasure, under the recognition of the Lord President of the Council, to co-operate heartily—first, with P. CUNLIFFE OWEN, Esq., the late Executive Commissioner, and subsequently with Mr. Owen's successor, Colonel SANDFORD, to both of whom their obligations are due for the aid afforded in obtaining the important concessions which have been granted to them by the General Commission of the Centennial Exhibition at Philadelphia.

In September last Mr. THOMAS COOK visited Philadelphia for the purpose of completing long-contemplated arrangements for the mutual accommodation of visitors to the Exhibition from all parts of Europe, and of those Americans who will be sure to avail themselves of unusual facilities for visiting Great Britain, the continent of Europe, the East, and other countries remote from the United States.

Applications were first made by Mr. Cook and Mr. Jenkins to the general managers and passenger and ticket agents of the various railroads which command the traffic of Philadelphia; and on the faith of their friendly assurances of co-operation, application was made to the chiefs, and the active Executive of the Exhibition Commission, for the grant of a site suitable for the erection of a large hall, to be used as a WORLD'S TICKET AND INQUIRY OFFICE, and for the exhibition and sale of articles manufactured in Palestine; and proposals were also made for permission to pitch tents, with camp equipments, illustrative of Palestine travel. These points have all been ceded : a most convenient site was allotted to us on the Exhibition grounds; an immense building is now nearly completed; permission has been granted to sell olive-wood and other articles manufactured at Jerusalem and Bethlehem, and the guide books descriptive of our tours, all, of course, subject to the payment of customs duties, according to tariff ; and in this WORLD'S TICKET OFFICE will be collected and offered for sale many thousands of travelling tickets and coupons. This will be an exhibition perfectly unique in its character, and offering facilities of travel in almost every part of the habitable globe. The European department will be under the superintendence of Mr. THOMAS COOK, whilst Mr. JENKINS, our American partner, will take charge of the home department, which has been planned and inaugurated by himself.

This being our position in America, the aim of this little pamphlet is to show how best to "cross the ferry," either to or fro ; how to live and how to travel on the other side, and how Americans coming to Philadelphia from the most extreme parts of the Union may avail themselves of trips to and through Europe. By the aid of our agents, from various parts and speaking various languages, we shall be able to direct those of strange tongues ; and by personal management of parties of strangers we hope to render good service to those who may lack confidence in their own power of dealing with those with whom they must necessarily come in contact, or may be deficient in information of the best places and the best things to be seen in America.

MAP OF ATLANTIC ROUTES.

Before proceeding to the details of Steamboat Arrangements of the various Companies, in whose behalf we are authorised to offer passage tickets to and from America, we invite attention to the new and beautiful map introduced into this pamphlet. In our several voyages across the Atlantic we have felt the want of a clear and well-defined route map, which would enable us from day to day to compare notes with the captain's figures of the mid-day observation, and by which the uninitiated might see at a glance their whereabouts.

This map has been executed by the famous map engravers, W. & A. K. Johnston, Edinburgh, with special instructions to show every degree of latitude and longitude by a single line; and the numerical divisions not to exceed five degrees. We also show, on the different parallels of latitude, the number of miles to a degree, this being a point on which many are confused. This is shown in a column on the right-hand side of the map. The distances by various routes are inserted, and the telegraph cables, as well as the various steamboat lines, are clearly shown. The observant will be interested by the indications of the gulf streams shown by white lines. The Saragosa, or Grassy Sea of 260,000 square miles, is plainly indicated, and the celebrated Newfoundland Banks cannot be passed over without observation. The chief places on the coast and interior of Newfoundland, Nova Scotia, and New England, are more fully noted than in most small maps; and from Philadelphia, the Chesapeake Bay, and various familiar names of places "down South" are clearly noted.

The southern route of steamers, from Gibraltar to New York, by the Azores, is shown by a distinct red line, which looks remarkably direct from the Straits of Gibraltar to the American ports of New York and Philadelphia. Henderson Bros. send Anchor Line steamers regularly that way, and facilities are offered by them for round trips, going by the southern and returning by the northern route, or *vice versâ*.

The Allan Line from Cape York to Quebec is a pleasant summer passage through the Gulf of St. Lawrence.

As a whole this new map of the steamboat routes of the Atlantic cannot fail to be appreciated, and we intend to have it bound up in a nice little case, as a guide to Atlantic voyagers; and along with it we will also give our

NEW TOURIST MAP OF CENTRAL EUROPE.

As this pamphlet is designed for Americans and others coming to Europe, as well as for those going from Europe to America, we insert a copy of this Map, which was engraved last year for the purpose of showing the lines for which Tickets may be had at the WORLD'S TICKET OFFICE, Philadelphia, and at LUDGATE CIRCUS, London; but since it was engraved and printed many additional lines have been provided for.

STEAMBOAT BOOKINGS.

The following pages show a choice of ten or a dozen steamboat lines, for any of which we are prepared to accept deposits and register passengers for any of the dates of departure. We can accept deposits of £5 by post or otherwise from any part of Great Britain, Ireland, and the continent of Europe; also from Eastern places named on next page (9).

As soon as deposits are received for any line, or for any steamer, a report will be made to the chief office of the company, and the berth will be secured with as much certainty as though the order were sent direct to the company's office. It will be necessary to state for what class of berth accommodation is desired where several classes of cabin passages are indicated by the different prices named; and the names of depositors must be given in full. For associated parties the best possible provision will be made, and the lowest rates obtained.

Passengers can be registered and deposits accepted at any of the offices of THOMAS COOK & SON, in London, Ludgate Circus, and 445, West Strand; also at Leicester, Birmingham, Manchester, Liverpool, Leeds, Bradford, Edinburgh, or Glasgow (after May 1st), Dublin, Paris, Brussels, Cologne, Geneva, Nice, and Rome (until May 1st), and at several continental hotels. The list of offices and agencies will be found on another page of this pamphlet.

THE BOOKINGS FROM AMERICA will be fully explained in publications to be issued at our Centennial Ticket Office, Philadelphia; at 261, Broadway, New York; and at all our American offices. We do not in this pamphlet quote the fares the contrary way, as there are differences in amount and in the gold or currency principle adopted by the companies. All these points will be fully explained to inquirers at our WORLD'S TICKET OFFICE, on the Centennial Grounds, Philadelphia.

One thing we beg of our friends in connection with this business in the approaching busy season, viz., that they will be moderate in their applications for information, and after they have engaged our corresponding clerks and offices they will not deprive us of our only interest in the issue of tickets—the commission allowed to us by the companies on the passages that we actually engage. A word to the considerate on this subject will suffice.

With these explanations we respectfully invite attention to the following lists of lines, steamers, and fares, prefaced by a page of through rates from foreign places.

THROUGH FARES
BY
ATLANTIC STEAMERS AND CONTINENTAL CONNECTIONS.

In trying to show through fares from distant places by different lines of Atlantic Steamers, and each of those lines showing various rates, it is necessary to have the arithmetical calculations of readers, or a volume would be required to show the combined figures. We therefore give below a table of through fares to Paris and Brussels, which, added to the quotations from either of those places, will show the entire amount from any place named underneath to the American ports. To nearly all of the places undernamed we can send travelling tickets to Paris, Brussels, London, &c., and where we have no Agency to receive deposits, the amount of £5 on a single, or £10 on a double voyage, can be sent direct to our Office, Ludgate Circus, London, Orders being made payable to THOMAS COOK & SON, Ludgate Circus Post Office.

Tickets can also be supplied, by post or otherwise, from London for the journey from any of the following places to London, Liverpool, Glasgow, or any other British port of departure for America.

From	First Class.	Second Class.	Where Deposits May be Made.
	Fcs. Cts.	Fcs. Cts.	[Havre.
Lyons to Paris, Single Journey-	63 15	47 40	Paris Office, 15, Place du
Marseilles to Paris - - -	106 40	79 85	Hotel du Louvre et de la Paix.
Nice to Paris - - - -	134 10	100 60	Grand Hotel, Nice.
Mentone to Paris - - -	136 95	102 70	Hotel Grande Bretagne, Mentone.
Geneva to Paris - - -	76 90	57 65	} Geneva Office, 90, Rue
Lausanne to Paris - - -	64 00	47 80	} du Rhone.
Bale to Paris - - - -	64 05	47 70	Hoffmann, Speyr, & Co.
Turin to Paris - - - -	100 10	74 55	Hotel Trombetta, Turin.
Milan to Paris - - - -	117 10	86 45	Hotel Royal, Milan.
Venice to Paris - - -	154 45	113 20	Hotel Victoria, Venice.
Florence to Paris - - -	152 20	111 50	Hotel New York, Florence
Rome to Paris - - - -	190 25	137 90	Rome Office, 1B, Piazza di Spagna.
Alexandria to Paris, by Rubattino Steamer to Genoa - - -	369 00	277 70	{ Cairo Office, Shepheard's
Alexandria to Paris, by P. & O. Steamer to Brindisi - -	525 00	386 25	} Hotel.
Constantinople to Paris, by Austrian Lloyd's to Trieste, to Venice, &c. - - - -	517 00	374 50	[Circus. London Office, Ludgate
Trieste to Paris, via Venice & Turin - - - - -	186 90	137 00	Hotel Victoria, Venice.
Vienna to Paris - - -	190 60	146 25	} London Office, Ludgate
Munich to Paris - - -	124 80	96 85	} Circus.
Cologne to Brussels - -	26 10	19 50	Cologne Office, 40, Domhof.
Heidelberg to Brussels - -	59 00	43 25	} London Office, Ludgate
Munich to Brussels - -	106 05	78 00	} Circus.
Berlin to Brussels - -	86 00	68 50	

STEAMBOAT LINES FROM LIVERPOOL.

We have arrangements for booking passengers by about a dozen lines, seven of which are from the Mersey. This being the chief port as to numbers of lines, we first group, in alphabetical order, the Liverpool companies and their arrangements, showing on one page their several fleets of steamers, days of sailing, and other particulars, and on the opposite page the fares charged from various points. Under this arrangement

THE ALLAN LINE

First claims notice. The steamers of this line are as follows (our space will not allow of our giving the names of commanders of vessels):

Sardinian	.	4376 tons	Prussian	. 3000 tons	Manitobau	.	2500	tons
Polynesian	.	4250 ,,	Caspian	. 3000 ,,	Phœnician	.	2500	,,
Circassian	.	4000 ,,	Nova Scotian	3200 ,,	Waldensian	.	2500	,,
Sarmatian	.	4000 ,,	Hibernian	. 3000 ,,	Corinthian	.	2000	,,
Moravian	.	3750 ,,	Austrian	. 2750 ,,	Newfoundland		1500	,,
Peruvian	.	3340 ,,	Nestorian	. 2750 ,,	Acadian	.	1500	,,
Scandinavian		3000 ,,	Canadian	. 2500 ,,				

The sailings of this line are weekly from Liverpool for Quebec (after 13th of April) on Thursdays, and fortnightly from Liverpool for Baltimore and Halifax on Tuesdays (on and after April 4th). Return tickets are available for coming from Quebec, Baltimore, or Halifax, and passengers can go out either way. The Canadian steamers take passengers from Londonderry the following day, and the Baltimore steamers call at Queenstown the day after departure from Liverpool. Berths are secured by THOMAS COOK & SON on receipt of a deposit of £5.

SAILINGS FOR QUEBEC.

Polynesian	- Thursday, April 20	Moravian	-	- Thursday, May 18
Sardinian -	- Thursday, April 27	Circassian	-	- Thursday, May 25
Peruvian -	- Thursday, May 4	Polynesian	-	- Thursday, June 1
Sarmatian -	- Thursday, May 11	Sardinian	-	- Thursday, June 8

From Londonderry the following day, returning from Quebec every Saturday.

SAILINGS FOR BALTIMORE, via HALIFAX.

Austrian -	- Tuesday, March 21	Nova Scotian		- Tuesday, May 16
Nova Scotian	- Tuesday, April 4	Caspian	-	- Tuesday, May 30
Caspian -	- Tuesday, April 18	Hibernian	-	- Tuesday, June 13
Hibernian -	- Tuesday, May 2	Nova Scotian		- Tuesday, June 27

From Queenstown following day, returning from Baltimore every alternate Tuesday.

Passengers taking "RETURN TICKETS" can go out by way of Halifax and Baltimore, and return by way of the St. Lawrence, or *vice versâ*, thus enabling them to see all places of interest between Baltimore and Quebec, without having to retrace their steps over any part of the journey. The Canadian Lakes (Lake of the Thousand Isles, &c.) and the Falls of Niagara are on the route between Baltimore and Quebec. Visitors should not miss these magnificent sights when brought within their reach on such easy terms.

Mr. JENKINS, of the firm of COOK, SON & JENKINS, New York, the Centennial Exhibition, Philadelphia, &c., has prepared programmes, as shown at the end of the steamboat notices, for 30 different routes between Baltimore or Halifax and Quebec. The steamer fares are given below. Passengers have the choice, under our special arrangements, of stopping at Halifax, and proceeding from thence by next fortnightly steamer. The return steamers leave Quebec every Saturday, and call at Moville; and Baltimore every alternate Tuesday, calling at Halifax and Queenstown.

Through Rates to Quebec and Baltimore and back,

BY ALLAN LINE.

	Single.			Return.		
From Liverpool to Quebec or Baltimore—	£	s.	d.	£	s.	d.
Cabin fares	12	0	0	22	0	0
,,	15	0	0	25	0	0
,,	18	0	0	30	0	0
Intermediate	7	7	0	14	14	0

From London—
Same rates as above, with the addition of 29s. first class, and 16s. 9d. third class, each way.

	Single.	Return.
From Paris—	Fcs.	Fcs.
First class throughout, via Calais to London and Liverpool, and £12 berths to Quebec or Baltimore -	412.00	773.00
First class throughout, via Calais to London and Liverpool, and £15 berths to Quebec or Baltimore	497.00	848.00
First class throughout, via Calais to London and Liverpool, and £18 berths to Quebec or Baltimore -	572.00	973.00
Third class, via Dieppe to London and Liverpool, and intermediate to Quebec or Baltimore -	226.00	452.00
From Brussels—		
First class throughout, via Calais or Ostend to London and Liverpool, and £12 berths to Quebec -	399.00	748.00
First class throughout, via Calais to London and Liverpool, and £15 berths to Quebec or Baltimore -	474.00	823.00
First class throughout, via Calais to London and Liverpool, and £18 berths to Quebec or Baltimore -	549.00	948.00
Second class, via Antwerp, Harwich, and third class London to Liverpool, and intermediate to Quebec or Baltimore -	227.00	454.00

Fares from other places in France, Switzerland, Italy, Germany, &c., may be ascertained by adding the amount shown to Paris, Brussels, &c., on page 9.

THE AMERICAN LINE TO PHILADELPHIA.

This is the only line of Transatlantic steamers that sails under the flag of the United States, and is the only line that sails to and from Philadelphia direct. This is an advantage so far as the Centennial Exhibition is concerned, and the directors of the line authorise us to say that a railway ticket from Philadelphia to New York and back will be given by them, without extra charge, to all their first class passengers who desire it.

This company provide for their intermediate passengers a better bill of fare than for steerage passengers, and they also provide beds, bedding, and necessary utensils. But the only steamers on which this provision is made are the "Pennsylvania," "Ohio," "Indiana," and "Illinois."

THE STEAMERS OF THE LINE ARE—

INDIANA.	PENNSYLVANIA.
ILLINOIS.	LORD CLIVE.
CITY OF BRISTOL.	CITY OF LIMERICK.
OHIO.	

WEEKLY SAILINGS.

INDIANA, Wednesday, April 5.	CITY OF LIMERICK, Wed., May 10.
ILLINOIS, Wednesday, April 12.	INDIANA, Wednesday, May 17.
CITY OF BRISTOL, Wednesday, April 19.	ILLINOIS, Wednesday, May 24.
OHIO, Wednesday, April 26.	LORD CLIVE, Wednesday, May 31.
PENNSYLVANIA, Wednesday, May 3.	OHIO, Wednesday, June 7.

Return Tickets are good for 12 months.

Through Rates to Philadelphia and back,
BY THE AMERICAN LINE.

From Liverpool—

		Single. £ s. d.	Return. £ s. d.
Saloon berths	According to position of and number in state room, all having equal privileges in the saloon.	22 1 0 18 18 0 15 15 0	36 15 0 31 10 0 26 5 0
Intermediate (bedding, &c., provided)	- -	8 8 0	15 15 0
Steerage - - - - -	-	6 6 0	12 12 0

From London—

Same rates as above, with the addition of £1 9s. first class, and 16s. 9d. third class, each way.

From Paris—

	Fcs.	Fcs.
First class throughout, *via* Calais and London to Liverpool, 21 guinea berths to Philadelphia - -	626.00	1070.00
First class throughout, *via* Calais and London to Liverpool, 18 guinea berths to Philadelphia - -	548.00	938.00
First class throughout, *via* Calais and London to Liverpool, 15 guinea berths to Philadelphia - -	470.00	807.00
Third class, *via* Dieppe and London to Liverpool, and intermediate to Philadelphia - - -	254.00	480.00

From Brussels—

First class throughout, *via* Calais or Ostend and London to Liverpool, 21 guinea berths to Philadelphia -	650.00	1117.00
First class, *via* Calais or Ostend and London to Liverpool, 18 guinea berths to Philadelphia - -	560.00	990.00
First class, *via* Calais or Ostend and London to Liverpool, 15 guinea berths to Philadelphia - -	481.00	859.00
Second class, Brussels to London, *via* Harwich or Flushing ; third class, London to Liverpool, and intermediate to Philadelphia - - -	252.00	479.00
Second class, Brussels to London, *via* Harwich or Flushing ; third class, London to Liverpool, and steerage to Philadelphia - - - -	202.00	400.00

Fares from places beyond Paris and Brussels may be ascertained by adding the rates quoted on page 9 to the above fares.

PULLMAN DRAWING-ROOM AND SLEEPING CARS run on the Midland Line between London and Liverpool, and third class passengers by the Midland route have the carriages and compartments formerly occupied by second class passengers.

THE CUNARD LINE.

Our arrangements for this line are highly satisfactory, the Company having promised to allot berths as fast as the deposits come to hand, and for large parties they will give us assurance of accommodation if reasonable notice is given. Thus, for our advertised French and Belgian party going on the 13th May, by the "Abyssinia," as soon as deposits are paid the names will be registered, and berths allotted according to priority of payment of deposits. The arrangements for France will be concentrated on our office, 15, Place du Havre, Paris, and our agent there will be in direct communication with the Paris office of the Company, where instructions have been given to treat with respect and promptitude every application made for berths by any appointed steamer of the line. At Brussels, our Office, Galerie du Roi, will be the centre of operations for Belgium, where deposits must be paid ; so also at Cologne, at our Office, 40, Domhof. We urge especial attention to the Programme of our first Personally-conducted Tour from the Continent, especially designed for France, Belgium, and the French-speaking division of Switzerland, for which deposits may be paid at our Office, 90, Rue du Rhône. The Programme, printed in French, can be had at any of our Continental Offices. In addition to regular bookings by all steamers of the Cunard Line, we hope the special party announced for May 13 will be followed by other similar parties as the season advances.

The following are the

APPOINTED SAILINGS for APRIL, MAY, JUNE, and JULY.

The following or other Royal Mail Steamers are intended to sail from Liverpool, *viâ* Queenstown :

Bothnia, for New York	- Saturday, April 1	*Scotia, for New York	- Saturday, June 3
†Batavia, for Boston -	- Tuesday, April 4	†Batavia, for Boston-	- Tuesday, June 6
Abyssinia, for New York,	Saturday, April 8	Bothnia, for New York	- Saturday, June 10
†Atlas, for Boston	- Tuesday, April 11	†China, for Boston -	- Tuesday, June 13
*Russia, for New York	- Saturday, April 15	Abyssinia, for New York,	Saturday, June 17
†Samaria, for Boston	- Tuesday, April 18	†Parthia, for Boston -	- Tuesday, June 20
Scythia, for New York	- Saturday, April 22	*Russia, for New York	- Saturday, June 24
†Algeria, for Boston -	- Tuesday, April 25	†Java, for Boston	- Tuesday, June 27
*Scotia, for New York	- Saturday, April 29	Scythia, for New York	- Saturday, July 1
†Siberia, for Boston -	- Tuesday, May 2	†Algeria, for Boston -	- Tuesday, July 4
Bothnia, for New York	- Saturday, May 6	*Scotia, for New York	- Saturday, July 8
†China, for Boston	- Tuesday, May 9	†Batavia, for Boston	- Tuesday, July 11
Abyssinia, for New York,	Saturday, May 13	Bothnia, for New York	- Saturday, July 15
†Parthia, for Boston	- Tuesday, May 16	†China, for Boston	- Tuesday, July 18
*Russia, for New York	- Saturday, May 20	Abyssinia, for New York	Saturday, July 22
†Java, for Boston	- Tuesday, May 23	†Parthia, for Boston-	- Tuesday, July 25
Scythia, for New York	- Saturday, May 27	*Russia, for New York	- Saturday, July 29
†Algeria, for Boston	- Tuesday, May 30		

* No Steerage Passengers carried on these voyages.   † Passengers booked by rail to New York without extra charge.

It will be seen from the above that passengers going out by Boston steamers have tickets provided by railway to New York, and if application is made to us, we can add tickets to Philadelphia also, without extra charge. Holders of B, C, D, and E Tickets may return in Class A on payment of the additional fare of 30 dollars gold at New York. Early application must be made for return passage accommodation, which can be negotiated at our WORLD'S TICKET OFFICE, Exhibition Grounds, Philadelphia, or at our Tourist Office, 261, Broadway, New York.

SPECIAL NOTICE OF THE CUNARD COMPANY.

With the view of diminishing the chances of collision, the steamers of this line take a specified course for all seasons of the year :—

On the outward passage from Queenstown to New York or Boston, crossing meridian of 50 at 43 lat., or nothing to the north of 43.

On the homeward passage, crossing the meridian of 50 at 42 lat., or nothing to the north of 42.

Through Rates to New York and Boston and back, BY CUNARD LINE.

	Single. £ s. d.	Return. £ s. d.
From Liverpool to New York.		
(A) First Class, by steamers carrying no steerage passengers	26 0 0	45 0 0
(B) Second class in same class of steamers	18 0 0	31 10 0
From Liverpool to Boston and New York, by other Cunard Steamers—		
(C) Best berths (two passengers in room)	22 1 0	31 10 0
(D) Ditto (three ,, ,,)	17 17 0	31 10 0
(E) Ditto (four ,, ,,)	15 15 0	31 10 0

N.B.—There are also two and three berthed rooms at the lower rates to suit families.

From London—

Same rates as above, with addition of 29s. first class, or 16s. 9d.* third class, each way.

From Paris—

	Fcs.	Fcs.
First class, *via* Calais to London and Liverpool, and A class of berths to New York	725.00	1338.00
Second class throughout, *via* Calais and London to Liverpool, and B class of berths to New York	528.00	942.00
First class, *via* Calais and London to Liverpool, and C class of berths to New York	625.00	1000.00
First class throughout, *via* Calais and London to Liverpool, and D class of berths to Boston or New York	550.00	1000.00
First class throughout, *via* Calais and London to Liverpool, and E class of berths to Boston or New York	500.00	1000.00

From Brussels—

First class throughout, *via* Calais to London and Liverpool, and A class of berths to New York	750.00	1324.00
First class, *via* † Ostend to London and Liverpool, and B class of berths to New York	545.00	977.00
First class, *via* † Ostend to London and Liverpool, and C class of berths to New York	620.00	977.00
First class, *via* † Ostend to London and Liverpool, and D class of berths to Boston or New York	541·00	977.00
First class, *via* † Ostend to London and Liverpool, and E class of berths to Boston or New York	489.00	977.00

* Third Class Passengers by Midland line, between London and Liverpool, have the same carriage accommodation as was formerly given to second class, the second class fare having been withdrawn, and first class fares reduced to nearly the former fare of second class.

PULLMAN DRAWING-ROOM CARS between London and Liverpool are charged 5s. extra. Sleeping berths, 6s. extra, by train leaving London at midnight.

† Passengers wishing to travel by Harwich or Flushing to London will have the difference of fare allowed.

THE INMAN LINE.

On the principle of "first love," we have a strong attachment to the Inman Line. Our first organising trip across the Atlantic was made by this line in November, 1865, and a section of our first special party for a tour in America went by the same line in May, 1866, the other division of the party going by the Anchor Line. A strong westerly gale of opposition blighted our hopes in the spring of 1866, but several of our associated parties from America have come by that line, and we are glad to incorporate it in our Centennial Arrangements, though we are a little restricted in our continental connections at Paris, from which point we are not in a position to quote through fares. But on the basis of our Liverpool, London, or Brussels rates, we can register passengers from any point, they paying the connecting fares from any place to those points. We insert the names of the steamers of the line, amongst which are some of the fastest that cross the Atlantic ; we also append the list of sailings to the end of August. On receipt of deposits we shall at once secure berths for any of the undermentioned steamers.

INMAN ROYAL MAIL STEAMERS.

SAILINGS from LIVERPOOL, via QUEENSTOWN, to NEW YORK.

City of Montreal - Thursday, Apr. 6	City of Berlin - - Thursday, July 20
City of Paris - - Thursday, Apr. 13	City of Montreal - Thursday, July 27
City of Chester - Thursday, Apr. 20	City of Chester - Thursday, Aug. 3
City of Richmond - Thursday, Apr. 27	City of Richmond - Thursday, Aug. 10
City of Brooklyn - Thursday, May 4	City of Brooklyn - Thursday, Aug. 17
City of Berlin - - Thursday, May 11	City of Berlin - - Thursday, Aug. 24
City of Montreal - Thursday, May 18	City of Montreal - Thursday, Aug. 31
City of Chester - Thursday, May 25	City of Chester - Thursday, Sept. 7
City of Richmond - Thursday, June 1	City of Richmond - Thursday, Sept. 14
City of Brooklyn - Thursday, June 8	City of Brooklyn - Thursday, Sept. 21
City of Berlin - - Thursday, June 15	City of Berlin - - Thursday, Sept. 28
City of Montreal - Thursday, June 22	City of Montreal - Thursday, Oct. 5
City of Chester - Thursday, June 29	City of Chester - Thursday, Oct. 12
City of Richmond - Thursday, July 6	City of Richmond - Thursday, Oct. 19
City of Brooklyn - Thursday, July 13	City of Brooklyn - Thursday, Oct. 26

Through Routes to New York and back, BY INMAN LINE.

From Liverpool—
Saloon berths, single, £12 12s., £15 15s., £18 18s., £22 1s. Return, £27 6s. to £31 10s.

From London—
Same rates as above, with the addition of 29s. first class, and 16s. 9d. third class, each way.

From Brussels—
First class. via Calais or Ostend and London to Liverpool, and saloon berths to New York, single, 415 fcs., 493 fcs., 572 fcs., 650 fcs. Return, 880 fcs. to 990 fcs.

Passengers taking the cheaper routes, via Harwich or Flushing, will have the difference of fare between Brussels and London allowed.

For through fares from various parts of Germany to Brussels, see page 9.

THE WHITE STAR LINE.

This is one of the lines for which we have long had authority to issue tickets on both sides of the Atlantic, and over which we have sent a good number of passengers. The White Star steamers are of the highest class, and the accommodation they offer is unquestionable in every respect. Saloons, state rooms, &c., are amidships in each of the steamers of this line. The Atlantic passage of our first personally-conducted tour round the world was made in one of them, and gave high satisfaction. Since then the "Adriatic," "Celtic," "Britannic," and "Germanic," have been added to the fleet, and we can, with the utmost confidence, commend to Centennial visitors the White Star Line. The sailings are from Liverpool, every Thursday, calling at Queenstown the following day, and from New York every Saturday.

Through Rates to New York and back,
BY WHITE STAR LINE.

	Single. £ s. d.	Return. £ s. d.
From Liverpool— According to state room accommodation, all having same saloon privileges, &c.	15 15 0 18 18 0 22 1 0	31 10 0

From London—
Same rates as above, with the addition of £1 9s. 0d. first class, and 16s. 9d. third class, each way.

From Paris—	Fcs.	Fcs.
First class throughout, via Calais and London to Liverpool, and 15 guinea berths to New York	505.00	1010.00
First class throughout, via Calais and London to Liverpool, and 18 guinea berths to New York	585.00	1010.00
First class throughout, via Calais and London to Liverpool, and 21 guinea berths to New York	663.00	1010.00

N.B.—Passengers travelling by the Dieppe route to London will have a reduction of 27s. on first class tickets for the single journey, and £2 on the double journey.

From Brussels—	Fcs.	Fcs.
First class throughout, via Calais or Ostend to London and Liverpool, and 15 guinea berth to New York	493.00	990.00
First class throughout, via Calais or Ostend to London and Liverpool, and 18 guinea berth to New York	570.00	990.00
First class throughout, via Calais or Ostend to London and Liverpool, and 21 guinea berth to New York	650.00	990.00

Through fares from distant places in France, Switzerland, Italy, Germany, Austria, &c., may be ascertained by combining the quotations to Paris or Brussels, as shown on page 9, with the rates quoted above.

THE DOMINION LINE.

By this line steamers are despatched from Liverpool for Quebec every Wednesday during the summer, and to Boston or Portland in winter. Special facilities are offered for round tours, by which may be combined any Liverpool, Glasgow, or other lines to New York or Philadelphia, either going to, or returning from, Quebec. Our arrangements afford facilities for combining railroads and intermediate steamboat lines between New York and Quebec, same as is proposed for the Allan Line, only that the latter, by their double system of working to Baltimore, Halifax, and Quebec, command the ocean passage both ways.

THE STEAMERS OF THE DOMINION LINE are—

DOMINION.	QUEBEC.	MISSISSIPPI.	ST. LOUIS.
TEXAS.	ONTARIO.	MEMPHIS.	MONTREAL.

The same Company, under the name of the Mississippi Line, also have a fortnightly service of steamers from Liverpool to New Orleans, for which we are authorised to book passengers at very moderate rates.

Through Rates to Quebec and back,
BY DOMINION LINE.

	Single. £ s. d.	Return. £ s. d.
From Liverpool—		
1st saloon ⎰ Three in state room	10 10 0	...
berths ⎱ Two in state room	12 12 0	21 0 0

From London—
Same rates as above, with the addition of 29s. first class, or 16s. 9d. third class, each way.

From Paris— Fcs. Fcs.
First class, via Calais and London to Liverpool, and
  10 guinea berths to Quebec - - - - 375.00   748.00
First class, via Calais and London to Liverpool, and
  12 guinea berths to Quebec - - - - 428.00   748.00

From Brussels—
First class, via Calais and London to Liverpool, and
  10 guinea berths to Quebec - - - - 362.00   723.00
First class, via Calais or Ostend and London to Liverpool, and 12 guinea berths to Quebec - - 415.00   723.00

Through Rates to New Orleans and back,
BY MISSISSIPPI LINE.

	Single. £ s. d.	Return. £ s. d.
From Liverpool—		
Saloon berths - - - - -	18 0 0	32 10 0

From London—
Same rate as above, with the addition of 29s. first class, and 16s. 9d. third class, each way.

From Paris— Fcs. Fcs.
First class throughout, via Calais to London and
  Liverpool, and saloon berths to New Orleans - 562.00   1035.00

From Brussels—
First class throughout, via Calais to London and
  Liverpool, and saloon berths to New Orleans - 550.00   1010.00

For either of the above lines passengers may be booked through from any of the places named on page 9, at the additional fares shown there.

THE GREAT WESTERN LINE.
From Bristol to New York.

This Line offers facilities for the West of England, and there are certain privileges granted of an exceptional character. One is, that passengers arriving the night before sailing are permitted to go on board and sleep in their berths, and as the boats lie alongside the quay they are easy of access at all hours. The steamers sail direct from Bristol to New York, not stopping at any Irish port. Bristol is only a journey of about three hours from London, and it is central for many towns and cities of the West. The fares, it will be seen, are very moderate, and there is a cheap second, or intermediate rate, for the working classes.

The following are the dates of sailing at present arranged for April and May :—

CORNWALL - - Saturday, April 22	SOMERSET - - - Saturday, May 20
GREAT WESTERN Saturday, May 6	ARAGON - - - Saturday, June 3

Through Rates to New York and back,
BY GREAT WESTERN LINE.

	Single. £ s. d.	Return. £ s. d.
From Bristol—		
Saloon berths .- - - - -	21 0 0	...
Second cabin - - - -	13 13 0	21 0 0
Second class, or intermediate - - -	8 8 0	13 13 0

From London—
Same rates as above, with the addition of £1 0s. 10d. first class, 15s. 8d. second class, 10s. 6d. third class, each way.

	Fcs.	Fcs.
From Paris—		
First class throughout, *via* Calais and London to Bristol, and best saloon berths to New York -	626.00	...
First class throughout, *via* Calais and London to Bristol, and second cabin berths to New York -	443.00	727.00
Third class, *via* Dieppe and London to Bristol, and intermediate to New York - - - -	245.00	410.00
From Brussels—		
First class throughout, *via* Calais and London to Bristol, and saloon berths to New York -	430.00	702.00
Second class to London, *via* Calais or Ostend, third class to Bristol, and intermediate to New York -	270.00	460.00

Fares from other places in France, Switzerland, Italy, Germany, &c., may be ascertained by adding the amounts shown to Paris, Brussels, &c., on page 9.

Passengers can be booked at our offices in London and Birmingham, on payment of a deposit of £5.

THE ANCHOR LINE.

The remark with which the Inman Line is introduced in this pamphlet applies also to "The Anchor." We began our American tours with these two lines, and the Anchor Company then gave us the cheapest special fare we have ever quoted to New York and back. Since that time the increase in the number, magnitude, and accommodation of the steamers of this line has enabled us to make special arrangements, such as no other company could well give. Twice have the company held for us the entire saloon accommodation of two of their best steamers, and on several other occasions parties of twenty to fifty have been provided for, sometimes in the very height of the season.

It has also been an advantage for American visitors, coming under personal escort, to come through Scotland, thus taking *en route* the Trossachs, the Highlands, the two chief cities, and the land of Scott, with all the pleasant attractions of Melrose and Abbotsford.

Under these circumstances, we naturally look again to the Clyde in prospect of the Centennial, and are in a position to treat advantageously for large or small parties desiring to go or come that way. The extra distance to the sea-board from the centre of England is met by a corresponding reduction of the ocean fares, and the journey from London to Glasgow is only a matter of ten or eleven hours. After the 1st of May we shall be in a position to offer a new tourist route to Scotland, a "consummation" that we have "devoutly" wished for many a long day.

In addition to the sailings from the Clyde every Saturday, and the usual call at Moville on Sunday morning, the Anchor Company offer facilities for a circular tour, going out by the coast of Italy, through the Straits of Gibraltar, by the coast of Spain and the islands of the Azores, to New York, as per line shown on our map of the Atlantic, and returning by the Northern Channel of Ireland and the Clyde. A party of Italians are preparing to take that route and make the circuit, and we have agreed to take them up at New York, conduct them through a great portion of the States, and then, on their arrival at Glasgow, give them a sight of Scotland and England, and take them back by Paris to Turin. Already a good number of the 150 provided for are registered. We have made several appointments for our travelling agents and staff to go out by the Glasgow steamers. Mr. ZIPPLITT on the 8th of April; Mr. RIPLEY on the 22nd of April (not the 15th, as erroneously stated in the *Excursionist*); Mr. FLOYD, from Jaffa, about the middle of May; and Mr. ALEXANDER HOWARD, of Beyrout, at a later date.

The following are the appointed sailings for April, May, and June.

FOR NEW YORK.

Bolivia	- Saturday, April 1	Elysia -	- Saturday, May 20
Elysia -	- Saturday, April 8	California	- Saturday, May 27
California	- Saturday, April 15	Anchoria	- Saturday, June 3
Anchoria	- Saturday, April 22	Ethiopia	- Saturday, June 10
Ethiopia	- Saturday, April 29	Victoria	- Saturday, June 17
Victoria	- Saturday, May 6	Bolivia	- Saturday, June 24
Bolivia	- Saturday, May 13	Calling at Moville next morning.	

Through Rates to New York & Philadelphia & back, BY ANCHOR LINE.

	Single.	Return.
From Glasgow or Moville—	£ s. d.	£ s. d.
Outside berths to New York - - -	16 16 0	26 5 0
Inside berths to New York - - -	13 13 0	24 3 0
Intermediate (with third class rail to Philadelphia)	8 8 0	14 14 0
Steerage (with third class rail to Philadelphia) -	6 6 0	12 12 0

From London—
Same rates as above, with addition of £3 5s. 0d.* first class, or £1 13s. 0d. third class, each way.

From Paris— Fcs. Fcs.
First class throughout, *via* Calais and London to Glasgow, and
  outside berths to New York - - - - 577 969
First class throughout, *via* Calais and London to Glasgow, and
  inside berths to New York - - - - 498 917
First class throughout, *via* Dieppe and London to Glasgow, and
  outside berths to New York - - - - 543 902
First class throughout, *via* Dieppe and London to Glasgow, and
  inside berths to New York - - - - 464 850
Third class, *via* Dieppe and London to Glasgow, and intermediate berths to New York and Philadelphia - 277 493
Third class, *via* Dieppe and London to Glasgow, and steerage
  to New York, and third class rail to Philadelphia - - 220 440

From Brussels—
First class, *via* Ostend or Calais and London to Glasgow, and
  best outside berths to New York - - - - 590 945
First class throughout, *via* Ostend or Calais and London to
  Glasgow, and inside berths to New York - - - 485 892
Second class, *via* Ostend or Calais to London, third class to
  Glasgow, and intermediate to New York and Philadelphia - 300 543
Second class, *via* Antwerp and Harwich to London, third class
  to Glasgow, and steerage to New York and Philadelphia 211 422

Intermediate and steerage passengers by the Anchor Line have to provide their own bedding.

* It is probable this fare will be reduced on the opening of the new Midland Line on the 1st of May, when accommodation equal to the old and discarded second class will be given at third class fares. Pullman Cars—"Drawing-room" by day, and "Sleeping" by night—will be also introduced.

For fares from other parts of the Continent, see additional table of rates to be added to the Paris, Brussels, or London fares, at page 9.

Saloon fares for the round trip from Genoa, Naples, Messina, Marseilles, Gibraltar, &c., to New York and back to Glasgow, vary, according to accommodation, from £30 to £40.

THE STATE LINE.

The service of this Line is at present fortnightly from the Clyde and from New York. The first departure in April will be Friday, the 14th, and then every alternate Friday, calling at Larne, Belfast, the following day. The return sailing day from New York is Wednesday.

The Steamers are:—

STATE OF NEVADA.	STATE OF GEORGIA.
STATE OF PENNSYLVANIA.	STATE OF INDIANA.
STATE OF VIRGINIA.	STATE OF ALABAMA.
STATE OF LOUISIANA.	

Through Rates to New York and back,
BY STATE LINE.

	Single. £ s. d.	Return. £ s. d.
From Glasgow—		
Saloon cabin berths	12 12 0	21 0 0
,, ,, ,, (selected)	14 14 0	
Second class	8 8 0	14 14 0

From London—
Same rates as above, with the addition of £3 5s. first class, and £1 13s. third class, each way.

	Fcs.	Fcs.
From Paris—		
First class throughout, *via* Calais to London and Glasgow, and 14 guinea berth to New York	525.00	838.00
First class throughout, *via* Calais to London and Glasgow, and 12 guinea berth to New York	473.00	838.00
Third class, *via* Dieppe and London to Glasgow, and second cabin berth to New York	273.00	543.00
From Brussels—		
First class throughout, *via* Calais to London and Glasgow, and 14 guinea berth to New York	512.00	813.00
First class throughout, *via* Calais to London and Glasgow, and 12 guinea berth to New York	460.00	813.00
Second class, *via* Antwerp and Harwich to London, third class to Glasgow, and second cabin to New York	274.00	545.00

Fares from other places in France, Switzerland, Italy, Germany, &c., may be ascertained by adding the amounts shown to Paris, Brussels, &c., on page 9.

The first class fares between London, &c., and Glasgow, will in all probability be somewhat lower, after the opening of the new Midland Line on the first of May. The old and, by the Midland Company, discarded second class accommodation is now appropriated to third class passengers. On the opening of the new line, Pullman Cars, "Drawing-room" for day, and "Sleeping" for night, will be run over that line.

THE WILSON LINE.

Our arrangements with the Wilson Line are two-fold: for Scandinavia and New York; and, availing ourselves of these arrangements, Through Programmes from Scandinavia to New York are in course of preparation, and it may be found practicable to avail ourselves also of their Russian service from St. Petersburg to Hull and from Hull to New York. In the Northern service there is a large fleet of steamers, and as we shall combine bookings for Norway, Sweden, &c., in connection with our Centennial operations from America, we give the names of the entire fleet, and also the service between Hull and Sweden and Norway.

WILSON LINE OF STEAMERS.

ALBION.	COMO.	HINDOO.	ORLANDO.	TASSO.
ANGELO.	DIDO.	HUMBER.	OTTO.	THOMAS WILSON.
APOLLO.	ELDORADO.	IRWELL.	OTHELLO.	
ARGO.	ERATO.	KELSO.	PACIFIC.	SAPPHO.
BRAVO.	FIDO.	LEO.	PALERMO.	URBINO.
CALYPSO.	GOZO.	MILO.	QUITO.	VIRAGO.
CATO.	HERO.	NAVARINO.	RINALDO.	XANTHO.
COLOMBO.	HIDALGO.	NERO.	ROLLO.	YEDDO.

HULL to SWEDEN and NORWAY.

To Gothenburg (carrying the Royal Mails).—"Rollo" or "Orlando," or other steamer, every Friday evening (weather and other circumstances permitting).

To Christiansand and Christiania.—The "Angelo," "Hero," or other steamer, every Friday evening.

To Stavanger and Bergen.—The "Argo," Thursday, 2nd March, and every alternate Thursday during the season.

To Drontheim.—The "Tasso," April 6th, and every alternate Thursday during the season.

From Hull and Southampton to New York.

Of the steamers above named, five are at present relegated to the New York service. These are the "Colombo," "Othello," "Eldorado," "Hindoo," and "Navarino." The sailings are at present fortnightly: from Hull, April 7th, 21st, and May 5th; and from Southampton, April 10th, 24th, and May 8th, and then every alternate Friday from Hull, and Monday from Southampton.

This being a new Atlantic service, and as we are specially interested in its success, as an adjunct to our Scandinavian arrangements, we sent one of our assistants to Southampton, to examine and report on the character of one of the outgoing ships, and he reports as follows:—

"The splendid steamers of this line are among the largest and most powerful vessels afloat, and are distinguished by the comfort and commodiousness of their passenger accommodation.

"The saloons of most of these steamers, in addition to being elegantly fitted with all modern improvements, are in the midships of the vessels, on the upper deck, and the sleeping-berths or state-rooms, which are large and well ventilated, are on the main deck, thus securing to the passenger the greatest amount of comfort and the least possible pitching motion in case of heavy weather.

"The saloon passengers' promenade deck of these steamers is also a special attraction.

"The second class accommodation, being also very commodious and comfortable, meets a want long felt by Transatlantic travellers desiring to combine the greatest degree of economy with a fair amount of comfort.

"Passengers of both classes are provided with a liberal table and good attendance."

Passengers from Yorkshire and Lincolnshire will find Hull to be a very convenient port of embarkation, and Southampton is the nearest port to London. From Paris, the nearest and most direct route is by Havre, but it will not add much to the expense to come from Paris to London by Dieppe, and then a short railway ride to Southampton.

Through Rates to New York and back, BY WILSON LINE.

	Single. £ s. d.	Return. £ s. d.
From Hull or Southampton—		
Saloon berths	⎧ 12 12 0 ⎫ ⎨ 14 14 0 ⎬ ⎩ 16 16 0 ⎭	25 4 0
Second class or intermediate	7 7 0	13 13 0

From London—
Same rates as above, with the addition of 15s. 6d. first class, 11s. second class, or 6s. 6d. third class, to Southampton.

	Fcs.	Fcs.
From Paris—		
First class throughout, *via* Calais and London to Southampton, and 12 guinea berth to New York	410.00	820.00
First class throughout, *via* Calais and London to Southampton, and 14 guinea berth to New York	463.00	820.00
First class throughout, *via* Calais and London to Southampton, and 16 guinea berth to New York	516.00	820.00
Third class, *via* Dieppe and London to Southampton, and intermediate to New York	214.00	400.00
From Brussels—		
First class throughout, *via* Calais or Ostend and London to Southampton, and 12 guinea berth to New York	397.00	795.00
First class, *via* Calais or Ostend and London to Southampton, and 14 guinea saloon to New York	450.00	794.00
Second class to London, *via* Calais or Ostend, third class to Southampton, and intermediate to New York	239.00	451.00
Second class, *via* Harwich or Flushing to London, third class to Southampton, and intermediate to New York	215.00	402.00

Through Fares from other places will be ascertained by adding the rates quoted on page 9 to the Paris or Brussels Fares, and through tickets can be sent from London or Paris available for any of the places named.

Through fares from Scandinavia to Hull, and thence to New York, will be found on pages 41 to 44.

THE HAMBURG-AMERICAN LINE.

The sailings of this Line are weekly, leaving Hamburg on Wednesdays, calling at Havre and Southampton. We have authority to book passengers from Southampton at the following fares:—

Through Rates to New York and back,
BY HAMBURG-AMERICAN LINE.

From Southampton—	Single. £ s. d.	Return. £ s. d.
Saloon berths - - - -	- 24 0 0	45 16 0
Second class, or intermediate - -	- 15 0 0	

STEERAGE RATES.

Just as we were going to press with this portion of our Programmes, letters from several Companies apprised us that, at a conference of the North Atlantic Companies, it had been agreed that Steerage Fares should be raised to £6 6s. for single voyages to New York or Philadelphia, and £12 12s. for Return Tickets. These terms are not quoted in the foregoing tables of rates, but must be understood as applying to all the lines.

For Emigrant Passengers only there are small reductions on the London and Liverpool third class fares, and a larger reduction on the third class fares between London and Glasgow. But these concessions are strictly limited to *bonâ fide* emigrants, and are not available for ordinary steerage passengers. Emigrants booked at our offices will have the benefit of these reductions to Liverpool or Glasgow.

OUR RAILWAY CONNECTIONS.

In looking over the varied contents of this pamphlet, it will be seen that in almost all parts of the European continent, in various parts of England, and throughout the chief districts of Ireland and Scotland, we have arrangements with nearly all the railway companies commanding local, national, and international traffic.

In America, notwithstanding unaccountable opposition on the part of one or two railroad companies, our partner, Mr. JENKINS, has made arrangements with considerably over 100 lines, besides numerous steamboat lines. When at Philadelphia, in September last, we saw the chiefs of every company whose lines are connected with the city, and they all gave us the assurance of cordial co-operation; most of them afterwards signed agreements to supply all their local and excursion tickets for sale at our office, and several of them have advertised their intention of doing so, in the official pamphlets of the Exhibition. Our New York office has already in stock more than 600 forms of American tickets, capable of being worked into a thousand combinations; and we have over 6,000 varieties to take from Ludgate Circus. These, added to our steamboat tickets and vouchers, present an aggregate of more than 25,000 single ticket forms, which are capable of being worked into 100,000 combinations.

THE MIDLAND RAILWAY of England is the line which connects our Liverpool, Glasgow, and Bristol steamboat tickets. Of course, any who choose can take their steamer tickets to commence at the ports of departure, finding their own way there. But all our through tickets, from any part of the country where the Midland Company have a position, are by their route. After the 1st of May the new line to Carlisle will be opened, and then will come a further reduction in Scotch fares, on the basis of the 1½d. first class rate (with 5 %, duty added) of the Midland Company, thus reducing the old 70s. fare to Edinburgh or Glasgow to, probably, about 58s.; the third class, at the old penny a-mile rate, getting the accommodation of the withdrawn second class fares. We can then give tickets to Glasgow, by the Glasgow and South-Western Line direct, or by the Waverley and Edinburgh route. From the ports of Liverpool, Glasgow, and Bristol nearly the whole country will be open to our arrangements, without unseeming or unnatural hostility to any other railway company. THE PULLMAN DRAWING-ROOM AND SLEEPING CARS will be a splendid addition to the Scottish train service, and the extra cost of their accommodation will be more than counterbalanced by the reductions of first class fares. For these cars we shall also issue tickets, both in England and America.

ACCOMMODATION FOR VISITORS TO PHILADELPHIA.

Next to the question, "How to get to Philadelphia?" comes up the almost equally important inquiry, "How and where shall we live when we get there?" The solution of this question has been, for a time at least, the puzzle in connection with every Great Exhibition from that of Hyde Park, in 1851, to the Vienna Exhibition in 1873. In connection with the first of the series of International Exhibitions, it was the privilege of Mr. THOMAS COOK to co-operate with the gentleman of the Home Office who had been appointed by the Royal Commission to attend to the matter, and eventually that gentleman gave it up entirely to Mr. COOK's management; and of the 150,000 visitors taken to London under his special arrangements, none were necessarily unprovided for. Agents and houses in various parts of London were engaged, and there were more lodgings than could find occupants. In 1862 Mr. COOK engaged a large house as an Exhibition Visitors' Home, besides a number of private family houses for the more select classes; and altogether 20,000 visitors to London availed themselves of his arrangements, amongst whom were the chief delegations of superior workmen, sent by the Governments of Paris, Turin, and places in Germany. In 1867 Mr. COOK adopted the same plans in Paris, and took the entire responsibilities of homes for 12,000 visitors of all classes, besides providing for thousands more in hotels.

In September last Mr. COOK visited Philadelphia for the purpose of making arrangements of various kinds for Centennial visitors, not the least of which was the selection of homes for them in the city, as well as in other parts where there will be great influxes of tourists. The result of negotiations in Philadelphia was highly satisfactory, considering the uncertainties of the demands that will be made on hotel-keepers and the selected lodging-houses. COOK, SON & JENKINS have long had pleasant business connections with the proprietor of the COLONNADE HOTEL, which was being enlarged, and supplements added to it, to meet the anticipated pressure. Our ordinary hotel prices on coupons in America is $3\frac{1}{2}$ dollars currency per day—13s. in English money. At Philadelphia, 1 dollar extra must be paid during the Centennial season, and that may be paid in currency or by a supplemental coupon, which we will be prepared to supply; thus making the full price for superior hotel accommodation in Philadelphia $4\frac{1}{2}$ dollars currency, or 16s. 6d. in English money, or 20 francs 60 centimes in French, Swiss, Belgian, or Italian gold. This provides for any unoccupied rooms on the arrival of travellers, at least three full meals, and all attendance, no extras being charged in American hotels. The proprietor of the Colonnade has an immense extent of accommodation, and hopes to provide for all coupon-holders. It is, of course, advisable to give the longest notice possible, and this we will do on behalf of our visitors.

The following are some of the principal hotels in America, &c., where our coupons, at the daily rate of $3\frac{1}{2}$ dollars currency, 13s. in English, or 16 francs 25 centimes, are accepted ; and in all cases this provides for full accommodation for three meals, and in many cases four, with bedroom and attendance.

HOTELS IN AMERICA.

ALEXANDRIA BAY—Thousand Islands House.
ATLANTA—Kimball House.
BALTIMORE—Eutaw House.
BOSTON—St. James' Hotel.
CHICAGO—Sherman House.
CINCINNATI—Gibson House.
COLORADO SPRINGS—Manitou House.
DETROIT—Russell House.
FORTRESS MONROE—Hygia Hotel.
GREEN COVE SPRINGS—Clarendon Hotel.
HAVANA (Cuba)—San Carlos Hotel.
JACKSONVILLE—Grand National.
MONTREAL—Ottowa House.
NEW YORK—Grand Central.
NEW ORLEANS—St. Charles.
NEWPORT, Vt.—Memphremagog House.
NIAGARA FALLS—International.
NIAGARA FALLS (Canadian side)—Clifton House.

NIAGARA CITY—Queen's Royal.
PHILADELPHIA—Colonnade (Special Rates).
PLYMOUTH, N. H.—Pemigewasset House.
PORTLAND—Falmouth House.
QUEBEC— { St. Louis House. { Russell House.
SALT LAKE CITY—Walker House.
SAN FRANCISCO—Palace Hotel.
SPRINGFIELD—Leland Hotel.
ST. LOUIS—Southern Hotel.
TORONTO—Queen's.
WASHINGTON CITY—Metropolitan.
WHITE MOUNTAINS—{ Crawford House. { Twin Mountain House.
YOSEMITE VALLEY { Leidig's Hotel. { Clark's Hotel. { Miller & Coulter's Hotel.

HOTELS IN CHINA, JAPAN, AND INDIA.

BOMBAY—Adelphi and Byculla Hotels.
CALCUTTA—Great Eastern Hotel.
HIOGO—Hiogo Hotel.
HONG-KONG—Hong-Kong Hotel.

NAGASAKI—Occidental Hotel.
SHANGHAI—Astor House.
YOKOHAMA—Grand Hotel.

THE LODGING HOUSE AGENCY of Philadelphia is the most perfect that we have known in connection with any previous Exhibition. We can guarantee respectable accommodation in private houses, of the nicest and cleanest character, at 9s. per day, inclusive of breakfast and tea with meats, lights and attendance. Philadelphia offers house accommodation superior to almost any known city. Whilst most cities and large places average from 12 to 15 inhabitants in a house, Philadelphia provides a self-contained, independent house for every five to six occupants. The houses rarely exceed two storeys above the ground floor, and cellar residences are unknown. Every cottage of four or half-a-dozen rooms is generally provided with a bath, and all domestic and sanitary conveniences. Provision has been secured by the Agency for 15,000 visitors in this class of accommodation, and this may be increased, in cases of emergency, to 25,000.

THOS. COOK & SON are the European Agents of the Centennial Lodging House Agency of Philadelphia, and also sell the coupons entitling their holders to one full day's accommodation in a private house or boarding-house in the city of Philadelphia. This Agency, formed by the agents of all the railway lines leading to Philadelphia, and endorsed by the United States Centennial Commission, Board of Finance, and by the Mayor of the City, have contracts with householders in private houses and in boarding-houses for upwards of 15,000 rooms. Their agents will be found on every train entering Philadelphia, ready to direct holders of these tickets or coupons to the houses selected for their accommodation.

Coupons for any number of days, for either hotel or private lodgings, can be had with steamboat tickets, and the supply may be replenished, if exhausted, at the World's Ticket Office on the Exhibition grounds. Coupons not used will be taken back at Philadelphia, New York, or London, at a discount of 10 per cent.

WHERE TO GO IN AMERICA.

THE two last features of our American Centennial arrangements are shown in the previous pages. We have shown how, from every part of the European Continent, and from the more distant North and East, parties may avail themselves of our agencies at Paris, Brussels, London, Liverpool, Glasgow, Hull, Southampton, or Bristol, and how they may fall in with outgoing steamers at Queenstown, Londonderry, Moville, and Belfast. We have next shown how, and where, and at what cost they may be accommodated at Philadelphia and elsewhere, whether they prefer hotel or more quiet life, so far as Philadelphia is concerned. The next great question that arises is, "Where shall we go in America?" and the next, "How shall we travel?" To answer these and similar inquiries, we have built our Hall on the Centennial grounds, under the highest authority, and are about to send out a staff of well-informed personal advisers, equipped with such descriptive and practical guides, maps, &c., as may be required; and when inquirers have satisfied themselves as to the best routes and the best places to be seen, we shall be able to furnish tickets and coupons for their journeys at the lowest rates at which they can be supplied. We also offer to provide personal conductors to go out from Philadelphia with large, or even small, parties for long or short tours.

Thus the experience of 36 years of similar work at home and abroad will be applied to our operations in America. In the following pages we offer a few models of tours for consideration, and to some of them we append quotations of charges for travelling, hotel accommodation, and personal guidance and attention. But in a country so vast as America, including the United States and Canada, with so many important and rising places of attraction, we feel the necessity of advising those who know the country to make out their own programmes and itineraries, come to our offices and confer with our clerks or our principals, and then decide.

Our whole ticket system in America is elastic and pliable—no straitwaistcoat ticket-books, which, if broken, may be attended with loss; but a multifarious scheme of single coupons, which may be put up in covers or cases in any combinations to suit the convenience of travellers, and to be returned, at small discount, if not used.

On the Continent of Europe there are a few hard and fast lines of travel for which books of coupons are well adapted; but, with the exception of Italy, for which country a unique pass ticket is arranged, all our combinations are made up separately to meet the wishes of travellers, and generally in their presence. It is this plan which renders valuable the services which we are able to render to both travellers and railway and other companies. A ticket-clerk at a railway station or other booking office sells tickets, or books of excursion tickets, for so much each, but it is not the business of such agents or clerks to explain the uses and working of the Tickets, and were they interrogated on those points, a hundred to one but they would resent, perhaps offensively, such demands upon their time and patience. It frequently taxes the endurance of our best informed clerks, with all the assistance of intelligible maps, to "fix" inquirers for the routes they wish to take, and any number of letters have to be written to attain the same end. To aid in this difficult work is our main object in going to Philadelphia, and locating ourselves at the WORLD'S TICKET AND INQUIRY OFFICE, on the Centennial grounds.

Nevertheless, some models of arrangement must be shown, and we cannot do better than reproduce such as have had the test of experience.

A Book of Model Tours, to the number of 1,249 combinations, was published by our American house last season, and it is probable that a reprint may be required for the Centennial tourist season. Be this as it may, we shall be prepared with itineraries to include all chief points of interest from north to south and from east to west. We have a network of tickets covering Nova Scotia and New England; the Grand Trunk Line from Quebec and Montreal to Toronto and Detroit; the Great Western Line from the suspension bridge at Niagara Falls to Hamilton, Toronto, London, Windsor, and Detroit. We have also tickets for the St. Lawrence steamers and the Lake of Ontario, and out to the north-western islands of the dominion of Canada—a region of intense interest. We have steamboat tickets for Lake Champlain, the Hudson River, Fall River, and Long Island Sound. We sent an immense number of tourists last year to the White Mountains, and other places of interest in New England. On the Atlantic coast we have excellent arrangements for steamers from New York to Richmond and intermediate ports, and the rivers, bays, &c., connecting Baltimore, Washington, and other places on or near the coast, with railroad connections also to the same districts. Western Virginia is rich in natural scenery, romantic caves, natural bridges, &c., for all of which we can provide. Pittsburg, Cincinnati, the Oil Regions, the Ohio River, Kentucky, with its mammoth caves; then on to St. Louis and the vast region beyond, to Colorado, the Rocky Mountains, the Sierra Nevadas, California, the Yosemite Valley, and return by Salt Lake, calling at the "City of the Saints," and, still returning, over the great prairies and plains to Chicago, with extensions, if desired, to St. Paul's, Lake Superior, Minnesota, and other places in that region. All through the Central States, by rail, river, or lake, back to New York or Philadelphia. Mr. JENKINS, who will control the American department, has all these regions, and far beyond, down to Florida and Mexico, mapped out on his brain and photographed on his memory by personal observation, and he can tell strangers the way they should go, and, if necessary, send assistants to show them the way. In his judgment on these matters we have the fullest confidence, and shall be glad to work in conjunction with him in the interest of British and Continental visitors.

MODEL PROGRAMMES AND ITINERARIES.

Some of the following are fixed arrangements for Special Tours, whilst others are merely shown as geographical or topographical arrangements. The ALLAN LINE connections between BALTIMORE, HALIFAX, and QUEBEC, are very important, and they can be taken either way.

CIRCULAR TOURS
Available for Passengers by
ALLAN LINE OF STEAMERS,
LANDING AT
QUEBEC, HALIFAX, OR BALTIMORE,
AND RETURNING FROM THOSE PLACES.

Out by Quebec and back by Baltimore.
The difference in Fares refers to Steamboat accommodation only. *See* p. 11.

Tour No. 1.—Liverpool to Quebec; rail to Portland, Boston; Fall River line to New York; rail to Philadelphia, Baltimore, and steamer to Liverpool, or *vice versa*. £25 17 0; £28 17 0; £33 17 0.

Tour No. 2.—Liverpool to Quebec; rail to Sherbrooke, Wells River, Concord, Nashua, Boston; Fall River line to New York; rail to Philadelphia, Baltimore, and steamer to Liverpool, or *vice versa*. £25 17 0; £28 17 0; £33 17 0.

Tour No. 3.—Liverpool to Quebec; rail to Groveton Junction, Wing Road, through the White Mountains to Fabyan House, Crawford House, Portland, Boston; Fall River line to New York; rail to Philadelphia, Baltimore, and steamer to Liverpool, or *vice versa*. £26 7 6; £29 7 6; £34 7 6.

Tour No. 4.—Liverpool to Quebec; rail to Gorham; stage to Glen House, summit of Mount Washington; rail to base of Mountain; stage to Fabyan House; rail to Crawford House, Portland, Boston; Fall River line to New York; rail to Philadelphia, Baltimore, and steamer to Liverpool, or *vice versa*. £28 0 6; £31 0 6; £36 0 6.

Tour No. 5.—Liverpool to Quebec; rail to Portland, Rochester, Nashua, Worcester, New London; Sound steamer to New York; rail to Philadelphia, Baltimore, and steamer to Liverpool, or *vice versa*. £25 19 0; £28 19 0; £33 19 0.

Tour No. 6.—Liverpool to Quebec; rail to Gorham; stage to Glen House, summit of Mount Washington; rail to base of mountain, Fabyan House, Twin Mountain House, Wells River, Plymouth, Concord, Nashua, Boston; Fall River line to New York; rail to Philadelphia, Baltimore, and steamer to Liverpool, or *vice versa*. £28 11 0; £31 11 0; £36 11 0.

Tour No. 7.—Liverpool to Quebec ; rail to Gorham ; stage to Glen House, summit of Mount Washington ; rail to base of Mountain ; rail to Twin Mountain House, Wells River, Concord, Nashua, Worcester, New London ; Sound steamer to New York ; rail to Philadelphia, Baltimore, and steamer to Liverpool, or *vice versa*. £28 3 0; £31 3 0 ; £36 3 0.

Tour No. 8.—Liverpool to Quebec ; rail or boat to Montreal ; rail to Rouse's Point, Plattsburg, Saratoga ; Albany steamer on Hudson River to New York ; rail to Philadelphia, Baltimore, or *vice versa*. £25 11 0 ; £28 11 0 ; £33 11 0.

Tour No 9.—Liverpool to Quebec ; rail or boat to Montreal ; rail to Rouse's Point, Plattsburg, Ticonderoga, Baldwin ; steamer on Lake George to Caldwell ; stage to Glen's Falls ; rail to Saratoga, Albany ; Hudson River steamer to New York ; rail to Philadelphia, Baltimore, or *vice versa*. £25 15 6 ; £28 15 6 ; £33 15 6.

Tour No. 10.—Liverpool to Quebec ; rail or boat to Montreal ; rail to Rouse's Point, Plattsburg ; steamer on Lake Champlain to Ticonderoga ; rail to Baldwin ; steamer on Lake George to Caldwell ; stage to Glen's Falls ; rail to Saratoga, Albany ; Hudson River steamer to New York ; rail to Philadelphia, Baltimore, and steamer to Liverpool, or *vice versa*. £25 15 6 ; £28 15 6 ; £33 15 6.

Out by Baltimore, and back by Quebec.

Tour No. 11.—Liverpool to Baltimore ; rail to Philadelphia, Bethlehem, Sayre, Geneva, Niagara Falls, Toronto, Thousand Islands, Rapids of St. Lawrence, Montreal ; Quebec (rail or boat); steamer to Liverpool. £27 4 0 ; £30 4 0 ; £35 4 0.

Tour No. 12.—Liverpool to Baltimore ; rail to Philadelphia, New York ; Hudson River steamer to Albany ; rail to Saratoga, Schenectady, Niagara Falls, Toronto, Thousand Islands, Rapids of St. Lawrence, Montreal ; rail or boat to Quebec, and steamer to Liverpool. £27 13 0 ; £30 13 0 ; £35 13 0.

Tour No. 13.—Liverpool to Baltimore ; rail to Philadelphia, New York ; Hudson River steamer to Albany ; rail to Niagara Falls, Toronto ; rail or boat to Thousand Islands, Rapids of St. Lawrence, Montreal, Quebec, and steamer to Liverpool. £29 4 6 ; £32 4 6 ; £37 4 6.

Tour No. 14.—Liverpool to Baltimore ; rail to Philadelphia, Williamsport, Elmira, Niagara Falls ; rail or boat to Toronto, Thousand Islands, Rapids of St. Lawrence, Montreal, Quebec, and steamer to Liverpool. £27 4 0 ; £30 4 0 ; £35 4 0.

Tour No. 15.—Liverpool to Baltimore ; rail to Philadelphia and back to Baltimore, Washington City, White Sulphur Springs, Huntington ; steamer on Ohio River to Cincinnati ; St. Louis, Chicago, Detroit, Niagara Falls; rail or boat to Toronto, Thousand Islands, Rapids of St. Lawrence, Montreal, Quebec ; steamer to Liverpool. £32 16 6 ; £35 16 6 ; £40 16 6.

Out by Baltimore and back by Halifax.

Tour No. 16.—Liverpool steamer to Baltimore ; rail to Philadelphia, New York ; Fall River line to Boston ; rail to Portland, Bangor, St. John ; Bay of Fundy steamer to Windsor; rail to Halifax, and steamer to Liverpool, or *vice versa*. £26 14 0 ; £29 14 0 ; £34 14 0.

Tour No. 17.—Liverpool steamer to Baltimore ; rail to Philadelphia, New York ; Fall River line to Boston ; rail to Portland, Bangor, St. John, Halifax, and steamer to Liverpool, or *vice versa*. £26 17 0 ; £29 17 0 ; £34 17 0.

Tour No. 18.—Liverpool steamer to Baltimore ; rail to Philadelphia, New York ; Hudson River steamer to Albany ; rail to Saratoga, Montreal ; rail or boat to Quebec ; boat through Gulf of St. Lawrence to Halifax, and steamer to Liverpool, or *vice versa*. £28 5 0 ; £31 5 0 ; £36 5 0.

Tour No. 19.—Liverpool steamer to Baltimore ; rail to Philadelphia, New York ; Hudson River steamer to Albany ; rail to Saratoga, Lake George ; steamer on Lake Champlain to Plattsburg ; rail to Montreal ; rail or boat to Quebec ; boat on Gulf of St. Lawrence to Halifax, and steamer to Liverpool, or *vice versa*. £29 1 0 ; £32 1 0 ; £37 1 0.

Tour No. 20.—Liverpool to Baltimore ; rail to Philadelphia, Sayre, Geneva, Niagara Falls, Toronto ; rail or boat to Thousand Islands, Rapids of St. Lawrence, Montreal, Quebec ; boat on Gulf of St. Lawrence to Halifax, and steamer to Liverpool. £29 18 0 ; £32 18 0; £37 18 0.

Tour No. 21.—Liverpool to Baltimore ; rail to Philadelphia, Sayre, Geneva, Niagara Falls, Toronto ; rail or boat to Thousand Islands, Rapids of St. Lawrence, Montreal ; rail to Wells River, Concord, Nashua, Boston, Portland, Bangor, St. John, Halifax, and steamer to Liverpool. £22 6 0 ; £25 6 0 ; £30 6 0.

Tour No. 22.—Liverpool to Baltimore ; rail to Philadelphia, Williamsport, Niagara Falls, Toronto ; rail or boat to Thousand Islands, Montreal, Newport, Wells River, White Mountains, North Conway, Portland, Bangor, St. John, Bay of Fundy, Halifax, and steamer to Liverpool. £31 10 0 ; £34 10 0 ; £39 10 0.

Tour No. 23.—Liverpool to Baltimore ; rail to Philadelphia, New York ; Hudson River steamer to Albany ; rail to Saratoga, Niagara Falls, Toronto ; rail or boat to Thousand Islands, Rapids of St. Lawrence, Montreal, Quebec ; boat on Gulf of St. Lawrence to Halifax, and steamer to Liverpool. £30 10 6 ; £33 10 6 ; £38 10 6.

Tour No. 24.—Liverpool to Baltimore ; rail to Philadelphia, New York ; Hudson River steamer to Albany; rail to Saratoga, Niagara Falls, Toronto ; rail or boat to Thousand Islands, Rapids of St. Lawrence, Montreal ; rail to Sherbrooke, White Mountains, Crawford House, North Conway, Portland, Bangor, St. John, Halifax, and steamer to Liverpool. £32 10 0 ; £35 10 0 ; £40 10 0.

Tour No. 25.—Liverpool to Baltimore; rail to Philadelphia, Washington City, Gordonsville, Huntington, Cincinnati, St. Louis, Chicago, Detroit, Niagara Falls, Toronto; rail or boat to Thousand Islands, Rapids of St. Lawrence, Montreal, Quebec; boat on Gulf of St. Lawrence to Halifax, and steamer to Liverpool. £35 18 0; £38 18 0; £43 18 0.

Out by Halifax and back by Quebec.

Tour No. 26.—Liverpool to Halifax; rail to Windsor; steamer on Bay of Fundy to St. John; rail to Bangor, Portland, Boston; Fall River line to New York; rail to Philadelphia, Sayre, Geneva, Niagara Falls, Toronto; rail or boat to Thousand Islands, Rapids of St. Lawrence, Montreal, Quebec, and steamer to Liverpool. £31 3 0; £34 3 0; £39 3 0.

Tour No. 27.—Liverpool to Halifax; rail to St. John, Bangor, Portland, Boston; Fall River line to New York; rail to Philadelphia, Baltimore, Washington, Cincinnati, St. Louis, Chicago, Detroit, Niagara Falls, Toronto; rail or boat to Thousand Islands, Rapids of St. Lawrence, Montreal, Quebec, and steamer to Liverpool. £36 11 6; £39 11 6; £44 11 6.

Tour No. 28.—Liverpool to Halifax; rail to St. John, Bangor, Portland, Boston; Fall River line to New York; rail to Philadelphia, New York; Hudson River steamer to Albany; rail to Saratoga, Niagara Falls, Toronto; rail or boat to Thousand Islands, Rapids of St. Lawrence, Montreal, Quebec, and steamer to Liverpool. £31 19 0; £34 19 0; £39 19 0.

Tour No. 29.—Liverpool to Halifax; rail to St. John, Bangor, Portland, Boston; Fall River line to New York; rail to Philadelphia, New York, Hudson River; steamer to Albany; rail to Saratoga, Plattsburg, Montreal; rail or boat to Quebec, and steamer to Liverpool, or *vice versa*. £29 10 0; £32 10 0; £37 10 0.

Tour No. 30.—Liverpool to Halifax; rail to St. John, Bangor, Portland, Gorham; stage to Glen House, summit of Mount Washington; rail to base; stage to Fabyan House, Crawford House, North Conway, Boston; Fall River line to New York; rail to Philadelphia, New York; boat on Hudson to Albany; rail to Saratoga, Niagara Falls, Toronto; rail or boat to Toronto, Thousand Islands, Montreal, Quebec, and steamer to Liverpool. £36 16 0; £39 16 0; £44 16 0.

The above are only given as specimens of some of the Tours which can be made in connection with Cook's American Tourist Tickets, which are of such an elastic character that they can be extended to almost any part of America. The above tours can be arranged so as to include Colorado, the Rocky Mountains, and California, should any wish to extend their time.

TOUR FROM FRANCE AND BELGIUM.

This is a special through arrangement from the Continent, designed for France and French-speaking people in Belgium, Switzerland, &c. We give the Programme in the French language, commencing on next page.

VOYAGES COOK
à L'Exposition du Centenaire de l'Indépendance Américaine à Philadelphie.

PROGRAMME
DES VOYAGES SPÉCIAUX
À L'EXPOSITION
DE PHILADELPHIE

(DÉPART DE PARIS OU DE BRUXELLES),

Organisés sous la conduite d'un représentant français de MM. COOK ET FILS, auquel seront adjoints des guides interprètes, capables de donner tous les renseignements les plus exacts dans tous les endroits indiqués dans le programme.

Le but de ces voyages est de fournir aux voyageurs l'occasion de voir les villes et localités les plus importantes, ainsi que les sites les plus remarquables et les scènes les plus grandioses de la nature aux Etats Unis et au Canada; tels que:

LES CHÛTES DU NIAGARA, LE FLEUVE ST. LAURENT, LES WHITE MOUNTAINS, CHICAGO, ST. LOUIS, WASHINGTON, ETC., ETC.

Départ de Paris et de Bruxelles, via Londres et Liverpool,
LE MERCREDI, 10 MAI, 1876.
Départ de Liverpool, par le paquebot de la Ligne Cunard,
LE SAMEDI, 13 MAI, 1876.

LES VOYAGES SONT COMBINÉS POUR QUATRE ITINÉRAIRES.

Le prix de chaque voyage, sa durée et le détail de chaque itinéraire sont indiqués ci après.

1er Voyage, durée 75 Jours -	-	Frs. 2800 00 cts.
2me ,,	,, 61 ,,	-	-	,, 2200 00 ,,
3me ,,	,, 54 ,,	-	-	,, 1950 00 ,,
4me ,,	,, 47 ,,	-	-	,, 1700 00 ,,

Les prix ci dessus comprennent le voyage en 1re classe sur les chemins de fer et sur les bateaux à vapeur, les frais de séjour et de nourriture dans les hôtels, les frais d'omnibus pour le transport des voyageurs et de leurs bagages entre les gares et les hôtels, les frais de porte-faix, les frais supplémentaires pour voyager en Amérique dans les wagons-salons et dortoirs, là où cela est jugé nécessaire, et enfin, les services du représentant et des guides pendant toute la durée du voyage.

ITINÉRAIRES.

PREMIER VOYAGE.

Mercredi, 10 Mai.
{ Départ de Paris (*via* Calais-Douvres ou Dieppe-Newhaven) pour Londres.
Départ de Bruxelles (*via* Calais ou Ostende et Douvres) pour Londres.

Jeudi, 11 Mai.—Séjour à Londres. *Grand Hôtel St. Pancras* (Midland Railway).
Vendredi, 12 Mai.—Départ pour Liverpool.
Samedi, 13 Mai.—Départ pour New York par le bateau de la Ligne Cunard.
Mercredi, 24 Mai.—Arrivée probable à New York. *Grand Hôtel Central*, New York.
Jeudi, 25 Mai.—Journée employée à voir les monuments de la ville.
Vendredi, 26 Mai.—Excursion en bateau sur le Fleuve Hudson, jusqu'à West Point et retour.
Samedi, 27 Mai.—Visite au Parc Central, à Harlem, High Bridge, etc.
Dimanche, 28 Mai.—Jour de repos à New York.
Lundi, 29 Mai.—Départ pour Philadelphie par l'express du matin.
Mardi, 30 Mai,
Mercredi, 31 Mai, | Séjour à Philadelphie—*Hôtel Colonnade*. Visite à l'Exposition,
Jeudi, 1 Juin, | les Mardi, Jeudi, Vendredi et Samedi ; le Mercredi,
Vendredi, 2 Juin, | jour auquel aura lieu la grande procession et revue des
Samedi, 3 Juin, | Knights-Templars, réunis au nombre d'environ 25,000.
Dimanche, 4 Juin.
Lundi, 5 Juin.—Départ et arrivée à Baltimore. *Hôtel Eutaw*.
Mardi, 6 Juin.—Départ en bateau à vapeur, par le baie de Chessapeake, pour West Point sur la rivière de York, et de là, par chemin de fer, pour Richmond, en passant par le champ de bataille de la dernière guerre de l'Union.
Mercredi, 7 Juin.—Arrivée à Richmond à 10h. du matin. *Hôtel Ballard* et *Hôtel de l'Echange*.
Jeudi, 8 Juin.—Départ de Richmond pour Quantico par chemin de fer, et transbordement sur bateau à vapeur allant à Washington par le Potomac. *Hôtel Métropolitain*.
Vendredi, 9 Juin.—Visite au Capitole, au Bureau des Brevets, à l'Institut de Smithson, à White House, etc., etc.
Samedi, 10 Juin.—Excursion au Mont Vernon, au tombeau de Washington.
Dimanche, 11 Juin.—Séjour à Washington.

Lundi, 12 Juin,
et
Mardi, 13 Juin.
{ Départ de Washington pour Cincinnati par la Virginie Occidentale, traversant pendant le jour le magnifique pays de Monts Alleghany et les Montagnes Bleues ; arrivée à Huntington sur l'Ohio. Transbordement sur le bateau pour Cincinnati.

Mercredi, 14 Juin.—Arrivée à Cincinnati à 5h. du matin. *Hôtel Gibson*.
Jeudi, 15 Juin.—A Cincinnati.
Vendredi, 16 Juin.—Départ pour St. Louis par l'express du matin.
Samedi, 17 Juin,
et } A St. Louis. *Southern Hôtel*.
Dimanche, 18 Juin.
Lundi, 19 Juin.—Visite à Springfield, au tombeau de Lincoln, et départ par le train du soir pour Chicago.
Mardi, 20 Juin.—Arrivée à Chicago. *Hôtel Sherman*.
Mercredi, 21 Juin.—A Chicago.

Jeudi, 22 Juin.—Départ de Chicago pour le train de 5h. 15m. du soir, en wagon-dortoir, pour les Chûtes du Niagara, en passant par le Michigan et le Canada.
Vendredi, 23 Juin, et }
Samedi, 24 Juin. } Arrivée à Niagara. *Hôtel International* et *Clifton House*.
Dimanche, 25 Juin.—Visite aux Chûtes du Niagara et environs.
Lundi, 26 Juin.—Départ par train du matin pour Toronto, et de là, par bateau à vapeur sur le Lac Ontario, pour Thousand Islands (Mille Isles) et les Rapides du St. Laurent, etc., etc.
Mardi, 27 Juin.—Arrivée à Montréal à 5h. du soir. *Ottawa House*.
Mercredi, 28 Juin.—Séjour à Montréal.
Jeudi, 29 Juin.—Descente du St. Laurent pour Québec sur le splendide bateau de la Ligne Richelieu.
Vendredi, 30 Juin.—Arrivée à Québec le matin. *Hôtel St. Louis*.
Samedi, 1 Juillet, et }
Dimanche, 2 Juillet. } Séjour à Québec, ville éminemment française.
Lundi, 3 Juillet.—Départ de Québec par train du matin pour les White Mountains.
Mardi, 4 Juillet.—Séjour à *Twin Mountain House*.
Mercredi, 5 Juillet.—Ascension du Mont Washington par le nouveau chemin de fer, dîner sur le sommet, et retour à *Crawford House*.
Jeudi, 6 Juillet.—Séjour à *Crawford House*.
Vendredi, 7 Juillet. — Départ par l'express du matin pour Boston, via Portland. Arrivée à Boston le même soir. *Hôtel St. James*.
Samedi, 8 Juillet, et }
Dimanche, 9 Juillet. } Séjour à Boston.
Lundi, 10 Juillet.—Départ pour New York par le magnifique bateau de la Ligne Fall River.
Mardi, 11 Juillet.—Arrivée à New York à 7h. du matin.
Mercredi, 12 Juillet.—Départ de New York pour Liverpool.
Samedi, 22 Juillet.—Arrivée probable à Liverpool.
Dimanche, 23 Juillet.—Séjour à Londres.
Lundi, 24 Juillet.—Départ de Londres et arrivée à Paris ou à Bruxelles.

Durée du Voyage, 75 Jours.
Prix 2800 francs.

DEUXIÈME VOYAGE.

Départ de Paris ou de Bruxelles, comme pour le Premier Voyage, jusqu'à Washington.

Lundi, 12 Juin.—Départ de Washington par un train du matin pour les Chûtes du Niagara. On traversera le magnifique pays des régions du charbon anthracite de la Pensylvanie.
Mardi, 13 Juin.—Arrivée aux Chûtes du Niagara. *Hôtel International*, ou *Clifton House*.
Mercredi, 14 Juin, et }
Jeudi, 15 Juin. } Aux Chûtes du Niagara.
Vendredi, 16 Juin.—On se rendra à Toronto par un train du matin pour prendre, sur le Lac Ontario, le bateau à vapeur qui mène aux Thousand Islands (Mille Iles) et aux Rapides du Fleuve St. Laurent.

Samedi, 17 Juin.—Arrivée à Montréal. *Ottawa House.*
Dimanche, 18 Juin.—Séjour à Montréal.
Lundi, 19 Juin.—Départ pour Québec, le soir, par le bateau de la Ligne Richelieu.
Mardi, 20 Juin.—Arrivée à Québec à 7h. du matin. *Hôtel St. Louis.*
Mercredi, 21 Juin.—Séjour à Québec.
Jeudi, 22 Juin.—Départ de Québec par train de jour pour *Crawford House*, en passant par les White Mountains (Montagnes Blanches).
Vendredi, 23 Juin.—Passé à *Crawford House.*
Samedi, 24 Juin.—Départ pour Boston, via Portland, par le chemin de fer, et arrivée à Boston. *Hôtel St. James.*
Dimanche, 25 Juin, et } Passés à Boston.
Lundi, 26 Juin.
Mardi, 27 Juin.—Départ de Boston, par chemin de fer, pour "Fall River," où l'on prend le magnifique bateau de la ligne de Fall River pour aller à New York.
Mercredi, 28 Juin.—Arrivée à New York, vers 7h. du matin, et transbordement sur le bateau à vapeur partant le même jour pour Liverpool.
Samedi, 8 Juillet.—Arrivée normale à Liverpool, et continuation sur Londres.
Dimanche, 9 Juillet.—Passé à Londres.
Lundi, 10 Juillet.—Arrivée à Paris ou à Bruxelles.

Durée du Voyage, 61 Jours.
Prix 2200 francs.

TROISIÈME VOYAGE.

Départ de Paris ou de Bruxelles, comme pour le Deuxième Voyage, jusqu'aux Chûtes du Niagara.

Mercredi, 14 Juin, et } Passés au Chûtes de Niagara. *Hôtel International.*
Jeudi, 15 Juin.
Vendredi, 16 Juin.—Départ par l'express pour Saratoga. *Hôtel des Etats Unis.*
Samedi, 17 Juin, et } Séjour à Saratoga (grande station balnéaire).
Dimanche, 18 Juin.
Lundi, 19 Juin.—Départ par un train du matin pour Albany, pour aller prendre le bateau sur le Hudson, et arrivée à New York le même jour, à 6h. du soir. *Grand Central Hôtel.*
Mardi, 20 Juin.—Passé à New York.
Mercredi, 21 Juin.—Départ pour Liverpool par bateau à vapeur.
Samedi, 1 Juillet.—Arrivée normale à Liverpool, et continuation sur Londres.
Dimanche, 2 Juillet.—Passé à Londres.
Lundi, 3 Juillet.—Arrivée à Paris ou à Bruxelles.

Durée du Voyage, 54 Jours.
Prix 1950 francs.

QUATRIÈME VOYAGE.

Départ de Paris ou de Bruxelles, comme pour le Premier, le Deuxième et le Troisième Voyage jusqu'à Baltimore.

Lundi, 5 Juin.—Voyage direct de Baltimore à Washington.
Mardi, 6 Juin, et } Séjour à Washington, visite des monuments publics.
Mercredi, 7 Juin.

Jeudi, 8 Juin.—Départ par le train du matin pour les Chûtes du Niagara, en traversant les grands gisements de charbon anthracite de la Pensylvanie.
Vendredi, 9 Juin.—Arrivée aux Chûtes du Niagara. *Hôtel International.*
Samedi, 10 Juin, et⎫ Passés aux Chûtes du Niagara.
Dimanche, 11 Juin.⎭
Lundi, 12 Juin.—Départ par train du matin pour Albany. *Delaware House.*
Mardi, 13 Juin.—Départ d'Albany par bateau à vapeur sur le Fleuve Hudson, et arrivée à New York à 6h. du soir. *Grand Central Hôtel.*
Mercredi, 14 Juin.—Départ de New York.
Samedi, 24 Juin.—Arrivée normale à Liverpool, et continuation sur Londres.
Dimanche, 25 Juin.—Séjour à Londres.
Lundi, 26 Juin.—Arrivée à Paris ou à Bruxelles.

Durée du Voyage, 47 Jours.
Prix 1700 francs.

AVIS.

Chaque voyageur à droit au transport gratuit d'une *seule* malle ou autre colis, dont le poids ne doit pas dépasser 40 kilogrammes. Tout transport de bagages supplémentaires reste à la charge de leur propriétaire.

Malgré le désir de rendre service aux voyageurs dans la plus grande mesure possible, en ce qui concerne le transport et l'enregistrement des bagages, MM. Thos. Cook et Fils ne peuvent accepter aucune responsabilité dans les cas de retard à la livraison, fausse direction, avaries ou perte de bagages. Dans tous les cas les voyageurs doivent s'assurer eux-mêmes de l'identité de leurs bagages, au départ et à l'arrivée, dans les gares et dans les hôtels. Ils sont aussi tenus d'assister personnellement à la visite des bagages par la douane.

Les arrangements conclus avec les hôtels pour tous les voyages faisant l'objet de ce programme sont les mêmes que ceux qui existent en Amérique dans tous les hôtels de premier ordre ; ils donnent droit à trois repas complets par jour, non compris les vins et les liqueurs. Selon l'usage Américain, les vins et liqueurs sont considérés comme des suppléments, et sont, en conséquence, payés par ceux qui les commandent.

Les frais de voitures commandées par les voyageurs, pour se rendre dans les lieux publics d'amusement, sont à leur charge, de même que le prix des entrées dans ces établissements.

Les guides interprètes mettront leur expérience au service des voyageurs qui désireraient faire des excursions en dehors du programme, afin de leur procurer les moyens de transport nécessaires et faire des arrangements aussi avantageux que possible.

DÉPÔT DE 500 FRANCS.

Les personnes qui veulent se faire inscrire pour un des quatre voyages du programme ont à verser, au moment de leur inscription, une somme de 500 francs. L'inscription doit avoir lieu avant le 15 Avril. Les places sur le bateau à vapeur sont réservées dans l'ordre d'inscription des voyageurs, les premiers inscrits obtenant les meilleures places.

Sur la demande du voyageur son dépôt lui sera remboursé, sous déduction de 20 °/₀, si cette demande est faite au moins quatre semaines avant le jour fixé pour le départ.

Dans le cas où les passagers seraient trop nombreux pour être tous admis sur le bateau partant de Liverpool le 13 Mai, les derniers inscrits partiraient par le bateau de la même ligne, Mardi le 16 Mai, et se trouveraient réunis à New York ou à Philadelphie avec les voyageurs partis par le premier bateau.

ON PEUT SE FAIRE INSCRIRE EN FAISANT LE VERSEMENT DU DÉPÔT DE 500 FRANCS.

A PARIS.—A l'Agence Générale de MM. THOMAS COOK ET FILS, Place du Havre, 15.
A MARSEILLE.—Au Grand Hôtel du Louvre et de la Paix.
A MENTON.—A l'Hôtel de la Grande Bretagne.
A NICE.—Au Grand Hôtel.
A LYON.—A l'Hôtel de l'Europe.
A DIJON.—A l'Hôtel du Jura.
A BORDEAUX.—A l'Hôtel de France.
A GENÈVE.—A l'Agence de MM. THOMAS COOK ET FILS, Rue du Rhône, 90.
A BRUXELLES.—A l'Agence de MM. THOMAS COOK ET FILS, Galerie du Roi, 22.
A ANVERS.—A l'Hôtel de l'Europe.
A LONDRES.—Au Bureau Central de MM. THOMAS COOK ET FILS, Ludgate Circus, Fleet Street.

NOTA.—Les voyageurs qui désireraient voir l'Utah, San Francisco et la vallée de Yosemite peuvent conclure, à cet effet, des arrangements avec MM. THOS. COOK, FILS ET JENKINS, à leurs bureaux de New York ou de Philadelphie. Dans ce cas, le billet valable pour le retour de New York à Paris ou Bruxelles sera prolongé pour une durée maxima de six mois.

A leur retour à Liverpool, les voyageurs ont la faculté de séjourner, à leurs frais, en Angleterre, tout en conservant le droit d'utiliser, quand bon leur semble, leur billet pour le retour de Liverpool à Londres et de Londres à Paris ou à Bruxelles.

On trouve des billets à prix réduit pour visiter l'Angleterre, l'Ecosse et l'Irlande, dans tous les bureaux ou agences de MM. THOS. COOK ET FILS, en Angleterre et en Amérique.

FROM ITALY

A similar Tour is arranged, but in three divisions, and an Italian Committee have the charge of the steamer arrangements from Genoa to Gibraltar, and from thence by the Azores to New York, as per line drawn on our Atlantic Route Map.

FROM SCANDINAVIA

We offer arrangements by the Wilson Line of steamers, as shown on next page.

COOK'S TOURS
FROM
SCANDINAVIA
TO THE
AMERICAN CENTENNIAL EXHIBITION
PHILADELPHIA, 1876.

Messrs. THOS. COOK & SON, having completed their arrangements with the principal Scandinavian railway and steamer administrations for Tours in Scandinavia, have now much pleasure in offering to the Scandinavian travelling public the advantages and economy of their world-known and popular system of tours, first, by

Personally-conducted Parties from Scandinavia to Philadelphia, &c., and back.

If sufficient encouragement be met with, Messrs. THOS. COOK & SON will, during the Philadelphia Exhibition season, have one or more such personally-conducted parties, the first to start early in June from Scandinavia to Philadelphia, including (for those so desiring it) a round tour, to return to New York from Philadelphia, via Baltimore, Washington, Cincinnati, St. Louis, Chicago, Detroit, Niagara, Albany, Boston, and Long Island Sound, New York, and spending five days in London on the way home.

Fares, including passage money and living in steamers and in hotels for 45 days, 700 and 1000 kronos. Fares being reckoned from Gottenburg, there will be a small extra charge for Stockholm, Christiania, Throndhjem, and Bergen.

The personally-conducted parties during the whole journey out and home will be under the protection and guidance of responsible conductors conversant with the Scandinavian languages, and are therefore especially recommendable to those not knowing the English language, and unaccustomed to travel, but most particularly to those accompanied by ladies.

In personally-conducted parties the conductor will pay all bills, and attend to the tickets and general travelling arrangements, and also give descriptive and guiding information in regard to the various places of interest along the route, so that the tourists by the personally-conducted parties are not only spared all the risks, anxieties, and cares of ordinary travel, but have in addition the gratuitous assistance of an experienced and responsible informant and guide in all matters of interest *en route*.

Personally-conducted Parties to Philadelphia.

The starting point for these will, of course, be Hull, that port forming the best point of confluence of the Scandinavian communications, and with the great advantage that passengers simultaneously leaving Stockholm, Copenhagen, Christiania, and Bergen, or Throndhjem, would, by the Steamers of the respective routes, arrive simultaneously at Hull, and thence, after a short rest on shore, at once proceed on the journey. The object in our exclusively choosing the WILSON LINE OF STEAMERS for our Scandinavian-American Exhibition Tours has been that we might thereby secure such arrangements as would, in all important matters, specially recommend said Steamers to the particular requirements and comforts of Scandinavians, and more particularly to parties containing ladies, while for those who understand the English language, and have confidence in their travelling abilities, we add the following List of Through Fares also by the WILSON LINE.

THROUGH RATES FROM PRINCIPAL SCANDINAVIAN CITIES TO PHILADELPHIA AND BACK.

ROUTE 1st.	1st Class all the way.	2nd Cl. & 1st Cl. American Railways.
FROM CHRISTIANIA, Stavanger, Bergen, via Hull, Southampton, New York, Philadelphia, returning same route	Kronos. 617	Kronos. 346
Including 3 days' hotel living in New York and 10 days' board in private house in Philadelphia	733	462

ROUTE 2nd.

From Christiania, Stavanger, or Bergen, via Hull, Southampton, New York, Philadelphia, Baltimore, Washington, returning by same route	636	365
Including hotel at New York for 3 days and 10 days at Philadelphia	752	481

ROUTE 3rd.

From Christiania, Stavanger, Bergen, via Hull, Southampton, New York, Philadelphia, Baltimore, Washington, Huntington, Cincinnati, St. Louis, Chicago, Detroit, Niagara, Albany, Springfield, Boston, Providence, New York, Southampton, Hull	795	523
With hotel coupons for 3 days in New York and 10 days in Philadelphia	911	639

Hotel coupons for Chicago can be had at 12 kronos per day.

43

	1st Class all the way.	2nd Cl. & 1st Cl. American Railways.

ROUTE 4th.
From Christiania, Stavanger, Bergen, *via* Hull, Southampton, New York, Philadelphia, Baltimore, Washington, Huntington, Cincinnati, St. Louis, Chicago, Omaha, Salt Lake City, Sacramento, San Francisco, Sacramento, Salt Lake City, Omaha, Chicago, Detroit, Niagara, Albany, Springfield, Boston, Providence, New York, Southampton, Hull - - - -   Kronos. 1659   Kronos. 1387

ROUTE 5th.
From Christiania, Stavanger, or Bergen, *via* Hull, Southampton, New York, Philadelphia, Washington, Cincinnati, St. Louis, Chicago, Omaha, Salt Lake City, Utah, Sacramento, San Francisco, Yokohama, Inland Sea of Japan, Shanghai, Hong-Kong, Singapore, Penang, Ceylon, Point de Galle (Ceylon), Madras, Calcutta, Bombay, Benares, Allahabad, Jubbulpore, Bombay, Aden, Suez, Cairo, Alexandria, Brindisi, Venice, Paris, London, Hull - -   4260

FROM STOCKHOLM or Throndhjem, as per Route 1st	680	365
With 13 days' hotel and boarding - -	796	578
By Route 2nd - - - - - -	699	384
Including 13 days' hotel and boarding in America - - - - - - -	815	500
Route 3rd - - - - - - -	858	541
With 13 days' hotel and boarding - -	974	657
Route 4th - - - - - - -	1722	1406
Route 5th - - - - - - -	4354	...

FROM GOTTENBURG, COPENHAGEN, STETTIN, DANZIG, MALMO, or HELSINGBORG, by Route 1st -	591	322
With 13 days' hotel and boarding - - -	707	439
By Route 2nd - - - - - -	610	342
With 13 days' hotel and boarding - -	726	458
By Route 3rd - - - - - -	769	500
With 13 days' hotel and boarding - -	885	616
By Route 4th - - - - - -	1633	1364
By Route 5th - - - - - -	4246	...

	1st Class. £ s. d.
FROM ST. PETERSBURG or RIGA, by Route 1st -	38 0 0
With 13 days' hotel and boarding - - -	44 9 0
By Route 2nd - - - - - -	39 7 0
With 13 days' hotel and boarding - - -	45 16 0
By Route 3rd - - - - - -	48 0 0
With 13 days' hotel and boarding - - -	54 10 0
By Route 4th - - - - - -	95 10 0
By Route 5th - - - - - -	236 0 0

N.B.—The above Fares also include living in North Sea, Baltic, and Transatlantic Steamers.

The foregoing Combined Routes are merely specimens, the fact being that we can issue Tickets for Single and Round Tour Journeys to all parts of the Atlantic and Pacific States, and in any form of combination that the traveller may select, and with or without hotel coupons.

Hotel coupons are sold only to those who have our travelling tickets.

The privileges of our World's Ticket Office will be accessible to *all* persons holding our tickets.

Passages for either independent travelling or by personally-conducted parties can be arranged for with any of the agents of Messrs. Thos. Wilson, Sons, & Co., or by letter written in English, or in the Scandinavian language, to our Chief Office.

At the Chief Office of Messrs. Thos. Wilson, Sons, & Co. in Hull, W. E. Bott & Co. and Thos. Cook & Son, London, may also be obtained through and return coupons for the above routes, and at the price as above quoted, if taken in connection with the Wilson Line of Steamers.

THOS. COOK & SON will, in Scandinavia, be represented by the Agencies of MESSRS. WILSON, SONS, & Co., in all matters concerning combined through rates of passage, &c., herein indicated.

THOS. WILSON, SONS, & CO.'S Agents:—

Throndhjem—Bachke & Co.	Christiania—H. Heitmann.
Bergen—Ole R. Olsen.	Gottenburg—J. W. Wilson.
Stavanger—T. C. Jonassen.	Stockholm—
Christiansand—O. C. Reinhardt.	Copenhagen—C. K. Hansen.

MODELS OF TOURS, STARTING FROM PHILADELPHIA.

The following Tours, in Three Divisions, have been already tested to a certain extent, and the Programmes are given here to show what may be done in thirty-two, forty-one, or fifty-four days. But these Tours can be arranged at pleasure, and they only constitute a small feature of our intended Personally-conducted Tours.

ITINERARY OF ROUTES AND NUMBER OF DAYS.

First Day, Leave Philadelphia by 12·15 p.m. train for Washington; arrive 5·15 p.m. *Metropolitan Hotel.*

Second Day, } At Washington; visiting Capitol, Smithsonian Institute, Patent Office, Treasury Buildings, &c.; Friday going to
Third Day, } Mount Vernon to see the Tomb of Washington.

Fourth Day, Leave Washington by Baltimore and Ohio Railroad for Baltimore by 8 a.m. express; dine in Baltimore; leaving by 4 p.m. boat down Chesapeake Bay for Richmond *via* York River route; arrive in Richmond early Sunday morning.

Fifth Day, At Richmond. *Ballard* and *Exchange Hotels.*

Sixth Day, Leave Richmond by Chesapeake and Ohio Railroad at 8·15 a.m. for Covington or White Sulphur Springs, arriving before dark.

Seventh Day, Leave Covington or White Sulphur Springs about 7 a.m., arrive at Huntington on Ohio River 5 p.m.; thus passing through the magnificent scenery of West Virginia by daylight; leave same evening for Cincinnati by steamboat.

Eighth Day, Arrive early in Cincinnati. *Gibson House.*

Ninth Day, In Cincinnati.

Tenth Day, Leave Cincinnati for Louisville by morning train. *Louisville Hotel.*

Eleventh Day, } In Louisville, giving opportunity to those who wish to visit
Twelfth Day, } the Mammoth Cave, at their own expense, to do so.

Leave Louisville by night train in Pullman Sleeping Cars at 8 p.m. for St. Louis, arriving 8·30 a.m.

Thirteenth Day, St. Louis. *Planters' Hotel.*

If at least 10 of a party have been booked for Colorado and the Rocky Mountains, or an additional 10 for California and the Yosemite Valley, a separate conductor will be supplied from St. Louis, where two, or, if necessary, three divisions will be formed; the first division to proceed to Chicago, the second to Denver or California, according to itineraries shown in the programme. Should there not be sufficient numbers to justify the employment of a conductor, tickets and hotel-coupons will be supplied to those who desire to go forward alone, and an equitable arrangement will be made for a return to the passengers of such just sum as may be proper, and included in the payment for incidental and other expenses necessary whilst with a conductor.

FIRST DIVISION.

Fourteenth Day, Leave St. Louis by Chicago and Alton Railroad morning express train for Chicago at 8·15 a.m.; passing through Springfield (the grave of Lincoln) at noon. Arrive in Chicago at 8 p.m. *Sherman House*.

Fifteenth Day, } At Chicago.
Sixteenth Day,

Seventeenth Day, Leave Chicago by 8·30 a.m. express, Michigan Central Railroad, for Detroit, arriving 5 p.m. *Russel House*.

Eighteenth Day, Leave Detroit, Great Western Railroad, 8·45 a.m., for Niagara Falls, arriving 7 p.m. *International Hotel*.

Nineteenth Day, } At Niagara Falls.
Twentieth Day,

Twenty-first Day, Leave Niagara at 12·35 p.m. for Hamilton and Toronto, reaching Toronto 4·40 p.m. *Queen's Hotel*.

Twenty-second Day, Leave Toronto by Canadian Royal Mail Steamer at 2 p.m. for Montreal, passing Lake Ontario in afternoon and night, reaching the Thousand Islands early next day, passing the rapids of St. Lawrence by daylight.

Twenty-third Day, Arrive at Montreal at 5 p.m. *Ottawa House*.

Twenty-fourth Day, At Montreal, leaving by 7 p.m. boat for Quebec.

Twenty-fifth Day, Arrive at Quebec early. *St. Louis Hotel*.

Twenty-sixth Day, to be spent in Quebec, leaving by night boat or train for Montreal.

Twenty-seventh Day, Arrive at Montreal for breakfast. *Ottawa House*.

Twenty-eighth Day, Leave Montreal by 9·20 a.m. express, Passumpsic Line, for Boston, passing through the White Mountains by daylight, reaching Boston in the evening. *St. James's Hotel*.

Twenty-ninth Day, In Boston.

Thirtieth Day, Leave Boston for Saratoga by day train. Hotel in Saratoga to be arranged.

Thirty-first Day, Leave Saratoga by early morning train for Albany, to take day boat on the Hudson, reaching New York at 6 p.m. *Grand Central Hotel*.

Thirty-second Day, Sail for England.

Any who desire can remain in New York during their pleasure, at their own expense; and upon notice being given at 261, Broadway, berths will be secured, and passengers placed on steamer free of any expense.

This arrangement includes First Class Railway travelling, sleeping and parlour cars when required, and hotel accommodation throughout the tour. It also includes porterage, omnibuses, and baggage-transfers from stations to hotels, and *vice versâ*. Baggage is limited to 100 lbs., which must be in one trunk or portmanteau. The incidental expenses are only included while the traveller is with the Conductor.

PROGRAMME OF SECOND DIVISION
TO
DENVER, COLORADO, SILVER MINES, ROCKY MOUNTAINS, &c.

Fourteenth Day, Leave St. Louis for Kansas City by morning express train, arriving at 10 p.m.
Fifteenth Day, Leave Kansas City by Kansas Pacific Railway at 9·50 a.m. for Denver, passing the great Buffalo Plains.
Sixteenth Day, Arrive at Denver at 6·30 a.m.
Seventeenth Day, ⎫
Eighteenth Day,   ⎬ To be spent at Denver, and in the silver-mining regions of the Rocky Mountains, during which time Colorado Springs will be visited. Programme to be arranged.
Nineteenth Day, ⎪
Twentieth Day,   ⎭
Twenty-first Day, Leave Denver for Cheyenne at 6·10 p.m., arrive 11·30 p.m.
Twenty-second Day, Leave Cheyenne at 2·50 p.m. for Omaha, viâ Union Pacific Railway.
Twenty-third Day, Arrive at Omaha at 3 p.m., and proceed direct to Chicago.
Twenty-fourth Day, Arrive at Chicago 3·15 p.m. *Sherman House*.
Twenty-fifth Day, ⎫ At Chicago.
Twenty-sixth Day, ⎭
Twenty-seventh Day, Leave Chicago by afternoon express train, Michigan Central Railroad, for Detroit, and through Canada to Niagara Falls.
Twenty-eighth Day, Arrive at Niagara Falls 1·15 p.m.
Twenty-ninth Day, At Niagara Falls. *International Hotel*.
Thirtieth Day, Leave Niagara Falls by early train to Toronto, arrive 10·50 a.m.; leave by afternoon steamer for Lake Ontario, One Thousand Islands, Rapids of St. Lawrence, and Montreal, passing all the fine scenery by daylight.
Thirty-first Day, Reach Montreal at 5 p.m. *Ottawa House*.
Thirty-second Day, ⎫ At Montreal; leaving by night boat for Quebec.
Thirty-third Day, ⎭
Thirty-fourth Day, Arrive at Quebec. *St. Louis Hotel*.
Thirty-fifth Day, Leave Quebec by day train for Portland and Boston.
Thirty-sixth Day, Reach Boston in evening.
Thirty-seventh Day, In Boston. *St. James's Hotel*.
Thirty-eighth Day, In Boston.
Thirty-ninth Day, Leave Boston by day train for Saratoga, reaching there same evening. Hotel to be arranged.
Fortieth Day, At Saratoga.
Forty-first Day, Leave Saratoga by early train to Albany, changing to day boat on Hudson River, reaching New York at 6 p.m. (*Grand Central Hotel*), where tour ends.

This also includes First Class Railway and Steamboat travelling, parlour and sleeping cars where required; meals and refreshments *en route;* and hotel accommodation.

It also includes baggage and omnibus, transfers from station to hotels, and *vice versâ.* Porterage and baggage is limited to 100 lbs., which must be packed in one trunk or portmanteau. These small payments are only included while the passenger travels with the Conductor.

PROGRAMME OF THIRD DIVISION
FOR
SALT LAKE, THE YOSEMITE VALLEY, CALIFORNIA, &c.

Seventeenth Day, Leave Denver at 6·10 p.m. for Cheyenne, arriving 11·30 p.m.
Eighteenth Day, Leave Cheyenne 1·10 p.m. for California.
Nineteenth Day, Arrive at Salt Lake City in the evening. *Walker House.*
Twentieth Day,
Twenty-first Day, } At Salt Lake City.
Twenty-second Day, Leave Salt Lake City at 3 p.m.
Twenty-third Day, Arrive in San Francisco at 8 p.m.
Twenty-fourth Day,
Twenty-fifth Day,
Twenty-sixth Day, } To be spent in San Francisco.
Twenty-seventh Day,
Twenty-eighth Day, Leave San Francisco at 8 a.m. for Lathrop and Merced.
Twenty-ninth Day, Leave Merced for Yosemite Valley.
Thirtieth Day,
Thirty-first Day, } To be spent in the Yosemite Valley, visiting all the
Thirty-second Day, points of interest, at the expense of the travellers.
Thirty-third Day, Leave Yosemite for Merced.
Thirty-fourth Day, Leave Merced for Lactross, Ogden, Omaha, and Chicago.
Thirty-fifth Day,
Thirty-sixth Day, } On Pullman Cars of Central and Union Pacific
Thirty-seventh Day, Railroad.
Thirty-eighth Day,
Thirty-ninth Day,
Fortieth Day, } In Chicago. *Sherman House.*
Forty-first Day,
Forty-second Day, Leave Chicago by afternoon express for Detroit, and through Canada to Niagara Falls.
Forty-third Day, Arrive at Niagara 1·15 p.m. *International Hotel.*
Forty-fourth Day, Niagara Falls.
Forty-fifth Day, Leave Niagara by early train to Toronto, and take 2 p.m. boat on Lake Ontario for the Thousand Islands; rapids of St. Lawrence and Montreal.
Forty-sixth Day, Reach Montreal 7 p.m. *Ottawa House.*
Forty-seventh Day, At Montreal.
Forty-eighth Day, Go to Quebec at 7 p.m. by night boat. *St. Louis Hotel.*
Forty-ninth Day, Leave Quebec by day (or night) train for Portland and Boston.
Fiftieth Day, Reach Boston in the evening. *St. James's Hotel.*
Fifty-first Day, In Boston.
Fifty-second Day, Leave Boston by day train for Saratoga. Arrive same evening.
Fifty-third Day, At Saratoga.
Fifty-fourth Day, Take early morning express train for Albany, changing to day boat on Hudson River, reaching New York at 6 p.m. (*Grand Central Hotel*), where tour in America ends.

This arrangement includes the same provisions as for First and Second Divisions.

A TOUR FROM SCOTLAND.

MR. JAMES PHILP, of the Cockburn Hotel, Edinburgh, is organizing a tour under our travelling and hotel arrangements, to start on the 6th of May. His circular shows two divisions—one for 20 days in the States and the other for 40 days. Terms and conditions may be known on application to Mr. Philp.

PERSONAL COMPANIONSHIP AND ASSISTANCE.

Our agents going out in April and May will be able to render all the ordinary assistance of personal conductors to those travelling under our arrangements and with our steamboat tickets.

The following are the arrangements for departure :—

Mr. ZIPPLITT, by Anchor Line, April 8.

Mr. RIPLEY, by Anchor Line, April 22.

Mr. FLOYD, from Jaffa (Line not fixed), May 20.

Mr. HOWARD, from Beyrout, early in June.

MR. THOMAS COOK goes by Cunard Line on the 15th of April ; returns from New York July 8, and leaves again for Philadelphia, August 28.

A TOUR ROUND THE WORLD

Will be organized to start from Philadelphia about the middle of September, and from San Francisco early in October, leaving time to see the Yosemite Valley.

Particulars and charges for this All Round Tour will be given in the *Excursionist*, published in London and America. The details cannot be given until Mr. COOK arrives at Philadelphia.

TOURS FROM AMERICA TO EUROPE AND THE EAST.

The design of this pamphlet, as originally planned, was to furnish full information of travelling arrangements from America to Great Britain and Ireland, to the continent of Europe, and to the East. But on reconsideration we have resolved to modify our plans, and to give only a few general notes of our arrangements as they apply to this side of the Atlantic.

In America, for Americans and others that may be coming eastward, it will be necessary to furnish information of our European plans in full detail, and another pamphlet, the size of this, may have to be published at New York or Philadelphia; and we therefore postpone till we get there the compilation of a new series of European programmes. But as we give a sort of bird's-eye view of our European Tourist arrangements in the map inserted at the end of these pages, we will, with all possible brevity, epitomise our travelling and tourist tickets for various countries.

IRELAND AND SCOTLAND

May be taken *en route* on the outward or homeward passage. In going out from Liverpool, any who choose may go in advance to Queenstown, to Londonderry or Belfast, and be taken up according to the line they have booked for; and in returning, it will be easy to drop off at any of those places where the steamers are appointed to stop, and make a short or long tour in the north, west, or south of the country. Our tourist tickets are arranged to cover the chief routes of the country, and especially the popular tourist districts, such as the Giant's Causeway, the Western Islands and Highlands of Connemara, Killarney, Glengarriff, Bantry, Cork, and other chief cities, such as Dublin, Belfast. Waterford, &c. Supplies of these tickets are kept at our American offices, at our London and other English offices, at our offices at Edinburgh and Glasgow, and for tourists going or coming through the country, at our Dublin office. These tickets are all issued at reduced rates both for railways and horse cars.

FOR SCOTLAND we have tickets covering all the best parts of the country by land, lakes, and sea coast. Parties embarking or landing at Glasgow have the easiest facilities for visiting Melrose, Abbotsford, Dryburgh, Roslin, Hawthornden, Edinburgh, Stirling, Bridge of Allan, Callander, the Trossachs, Loch Katrine, Loch Lomond, Loch Long, Dumbarton, and Glasgow; and if a wider range is desired, nothing can surpass in Highland interest the voyage down the Clyde, by Rothesay, the Kyles of Bute, Crinan Canal, Atlantic Coast, Oban, Staffa and Iona, Glencoe, the Caledonian Canal, Inverness, Skye, the Pass of Killiecrankie, Dunkeld, Perth, Aberdeen, and other famed places. For 30 years we have been working out Scottish tourist arrangements, and have a thorough command of the country. Our plans will be facilitated by the opening of the new tourist line from Settle to Carlisle, thus giving a through route from Leeds, Bradford, Manchester, and other Lancashire towns and cities, to Edinburgh by the charming Waverley Line, and to Glasgow either by that line or direct from Carlisle by the Glasgow and South-western route. By arrangement we can organise trips through the lake district of Westmoreland and Cumberland, and can also book to the Isle of Man by the shortest and most direct sea passage from Barrow.

To facilitate Scottish arrangements we shall again station our agent, Mr. CATES, at Edinburgh, with an assistant at Glasgow; and personally-conducted tours will be arranged at intervals during the season. It was in Scotland that Mr. THOMAS COOK laid the foundation of the tourist systems of Europe, by model arrangements that have been copied, or their principles embodied, in almost every European country, and have now extended to America. The excursionists and tourists travelling to or through Scotland under our arrangements go into hundreds of thousands. The happiest of our tourist work has centred there, and but for this great Centennial we should have been delighted once more to spend the best part of a summer in Scotland.

ENGLAND AND WALES.

With the great Midland system of railways as a centre of operations, we can now cover the land from the Solway and the Clyde to the extreme Western Coast, and from the lake district to the eastern and southern shores, taking in also the Channel Islands and the Isle of Wight. A most extensive system of tours was last year opened between Bristol and the Land's End, and along the Cornish Coast to Falmouth, Plymouth, Torquay, Exeter, &c., and we are now completing the connections of coupons over the whole of the routes, the extreme points of which we have indicated. There are very few important towns and cities that we cannot reach by positive arrangements. We work with or for the connecting lines of the Furness Railway, "oversands" to the head of the lake district. We have tickets from London to all parts of the Great Eastern district, the London Brighton and South Coast Lines; the London Chatham and Dover Lines; the Great Western, for South and North Wales, Devon and Cornwall, in addition to our own extensive series of western tickets. To carry out these arrangements, we have, in addition to our two chief offices in London, excellent office arrangements at Birmingham, Manchester, Liverpool, Leeds, and Bradford, besides numerous sub-agencies in other places—such as Leicester, Sheffield, Bristol, Newcastle-on-Tyne, &c.

OUR CHANNEL ROUTES include steamboat service from Leith, Hull, Grimsby, &c., to Rotterdam, Antwerp, Hamburg, &c.; the Harwich and Antwerp and Rotterdam Steamers of the Great Eastern Company; the new Flushing Route from Queenborough or Sheerness; the Thames

Steamers of the General Steam Navigation Company to various continental and northern ports; the famous Wilson Line from Hull or London to Scandinavia, &c. From London we have also command of the shortest sea routes, and the cheapest through routes to Paris, Brussels, &c. For all these continental points we can issue tickets from Dublin, Edinburgh, Glasgow, Liverpool, Manchester, Birmingham, Leeds, Bradford, and all other chief places on the Midland Railway. A list of our offices will be appended to these notes.

The travelling arrangements of our own inauguration on the Continent cover the whole of Central Europe, as partially indicated by the red lines on our European Map. But these countries must be briefly noticed in detail.

FRANCE.

We have already spoken of the various ways of getting to Paris, by both the Western and the Northern Lines. In Paris we have splendid arrangements for showing the chief places in the city and suburbs, by a four-in-hand turn-out, under the management and contract of Mr. PLAGGE, our office clerk, at 15, Place du Havre. From Paris we have the most convenient travelling tickets for long lines ever established, and all of our own arrangement, for Lyons, Marseilles, Cannes, Nice, and Mentone ; also for Bordeaux and other places in that direction. We have also our own through tickets, allowing numerous breaks by the way, for Modane and Turin, and for Geneva and Lausanne. All these tickets for travelling through France enable passengers to stop at Fontainebleau, Dijon, Macon, Culoz, Aix-les-Bains, Chambery, and Modane ; and tickets for Nice and Mentone allow breaks at Lyons, Marseilles, Toulon, and Cannes. Through France, in all these directions, 66 lbs. of baggage is allowed on each ticket.

SWITZERLAND.

We can reach Switzerland by our through tickets, as already shown, *via* Dijon and Macon, and we have also through tickets by the East of France Lines, *via* Strasburg and Belfort. Another route to Switzerland is by the Luxembourg Railway from Brussels, *via* Metz and the battle-fields of the Franco-German War. We likewise book by the Rhine route to Switzerland, *via* Mayence, Heidelberg, Baden-Baden, &c. Two excellent systems of Circular Tickets are issued in the season from May to October, connecting Paris with Switzerland by the most practicable routes. These tickets were first prepared for English travellers, in the English language, in 1863, by Mr. THOMAS COOK, and they have been greatly appreciated.

When Mr. COOK first visited Switzerland, in 1863, there was not a circular ticket in the country, except a dear and impracticable one combining Chamouny with the Lake of Geneva. Mr. Cook mapped out the country into a series of routes, and formed numerous ticket combinations, which were worked by us exclusively for ten years, when our contract expired, and a new system of single coupons, to the number or more than a hundred, was brought out ; and now the chief lines of the country are under our arrangements, the coupons being combined so as to meet the wishes of travellers. These coupons are for railways, steamboats, and diligences, the latter crossing the Alps by the Simplon, St. Gotthard, Splugen, and Bernardine to Italy. We also reach the Black Forest from Schaffhausen, and here a new region of interest has been brought under our ticket arrangements. We have a central office for Switzerland, at Geneva, where any of our Swiss, Alpine, and Italian tickets may be obtained.

ITALY.

Wonderful changes have come over the travelling arrangements of Italy since, in 1863, Mr. COOK first crossed the Alps to propose to the Companies then in charge of the railways and some of the coast steamers a system of Circular Tours. After much explanation and some pressure the proposals were accepted, and the first Circular Tourist Tickets ever seen in Italy were introduced by Mr. COOK early in 1864. But at that time the chief excursion business done in Italy was by organised parties, personally conducted by Mr. COOK and one or two friendly assistants, the numbers of the parties ranging from 50 to 100. Once in that first year 96 were carried over Mont Cenis in diligences.

Now all is changed : railways intersect and almost girdle the peninsula ; Rome is made accessible by nearly half a dozen lines, and a system of tickets is established on a most liberal basis, reductions of price ranging according to distance, from 30 to 45 per cent., and allowing fro 30 to 60 days in the country.

We have a great variety of these tickets, both for the country and the lakes, and not only have we a great supply for London and all our offices in Great Britain and on the Continent, but a special series has been prepared for the Centennial Exhibition and general American issue.

Our business is now chiefly managed in Italy at a central office in Rome, open from September to the end of April.

BELGIUM, HOLLAND, AND THE RHINE DISTRICT.

Our ticket arrangements cover the whole of these districts, from Rotterdam, Antwerp, and Brussels, to the Hague, through Holland and Belgium, and up the Rhine, or by its banks to the charming places of Rhineland. We also combine Rhine Tours with the Black Forest, Strasburg, and other places of attraction.

GERMANY, BAVARIA, AND AUSTRIA.

Our tickets combine almost every section of United Germany, Berlin, Dresden, Munich, Salzburg, Vienna, the Tyrol, and over the Brenner, or Semmering, to Italy. For these tickets, orders will be accepted at the WORLD'S TICKET OFFICE, and at all our other offices on either side of the Atlantic.

SCANDINAVIA.

Last season we commenced a system of tours to Norway, Denmark, and Sweden. An experimental special tour was made to the North Cape and through parts of Lapland. The difficulties of travel in these parts are great and peculiar, and we shall be very careful in all future arrangements not to attempt the impracticable. A system of independent coupons has been prepared for the Swedish State Railways, and we hope before the first of May to get it perfected and brought into operation. We have also effected arrangements with the Wilson Steamers, as well as those of the General Steam Navigation Company.

[SPAIN.

With the return of peace we hope to resume our negotiations, which were agreed upon before the war, for a system of tickets for independent travel and for tours in Spain.

THE NILE AND PALESTINE.

We have now had eight years' experience of tourist management in Egypt and the Holy Land. We have taken yearly up the Nile, by the Khédivic steamers, from 200 to 300 tourists. Previous to the late season we had not attempted to go beyond the First Cataract, but we have now extended our tours, by special steamer arrangements, to the Second Cataract. The season, as a whole, has been the most successful of the eight in which it has been our pleasure to serve the Administration of the Viceroy, and we have every reason to believe that additional facilities and improved service will be the result of the satisfaction expressed with regard to our agency for the Nile steamers.

OUR PALESTINE TOURS, including three or four each year personally conducted, besides great numbers of independent arrangements for small, select, or family parties, have comprehended at least half the travellers that have gone through the Holy Land. Two or three years since we inaugurated a system of cheap short tours for ten, twelve, or fourteen days, from Jaffa to Jerusalem, Bethlehem, the Dead Sea, the Jordan, Bethany, and over the Mount of Olives to Jerusalem; and that arrangement has proved very satisfactory to those who did not wish to go through to Damascus, Baalbec, the Lebanon, and Beyrout. We have also organised extended tours to the Desert, Sinai, Petra, the Land of Moab, and the Hauran. Many, both English and American travellers in Palestine, will recognise, and will be glad to meet at Philadelphia, our Eastern contractor, Mr. ALEXANDER HOWARD, of Beyrout, with his excellent assistant, Mr. ROLLA FLOYD, originally from Maine, faithful among the faithless colonists who failed in their attempts to establish an American colony on a grant of land conceded to them by the Sultan, and which has now passed into the hands of a German party.

From Mr. HOWARD and Mr. FLOYD personal information of Palestine Tours may be obtained, and the tents forwarded from Alexandria will show the kind of habitations occupied in the desert and in the land where the "father of the faithful" and his family and descendants lived in tents.

Aided by the tests of long experience, Messrs. HOWARD and FLOYD will be able to give sound information as to the requisites and costs of Palestine Tours ; and in addition to their personal testimony we will be prepared with printed programmes, itineraries, and quotations.

MEDITERRANEAN, ARABIAN, INDIAN, CHINESE, JAPANESE, & PACIFIC STEAMSHIP TICKETS.

For the Austrian Lloyds of Trieste, the Messageries Maritimes of France, the Rubattino of Italy, the Khédivie of Egypt, and the Russian Steamers of the Syrian Coast and the Black Sea, we shall be able to issue tickets or vouchers securing passages by any of those lines of the Adriatic, the Mediterranean, and the Black Sea, with extensions to Vienna by the Danube.

Our agency for the Peninsular and Oriental Steam Navigation Company gives us command of all the seas from the Mediterranean to Japan. We can book from Venice or Brindisi by this great line to Alexandria, Port Said, Suez (by the Canal), Aden, Bombay, Point de Galle, Calcutta, Australia, Penang, Singapore, Hong Kong, Shanghai, and Yokohama ; and from Shanghai also we can book over the Inland Sea of Japan, and from Yokohama to San Francisco, completing the circle of the world by railroad tickets to Philadelphia or New York.

These notes merely epitomise the compass of our arrangements, the details of which represent thousands of tickets and coupons.

PERSONALLY-CONDUCTED TOURS.

The system of personal management of tourist parties, inaugurated by Mr. THOMAS COOK in North Wales in 1845 ; commenced in Scotland in 1846 ; extended to Ireland in 1849 ; practised on the Rhine and round by Strasburg to Paris and London in 1855 ; actively carried out in Great Britain and Ireland until 1863 ; then worked out through Switzerland, over the Alps, and through Italy ; then embracing for eight years Egypt and Palestine, growing and increasing in its demands until carried round the world in 1872–3 ; has now resolved itself into a great system, requiring a large staff of intelligent, courteous, reliable men, whose services are engaged all the year round, and who will go to America as they are required, and return with Americans to England, and be ready to go forward to the Continent with any who want their aid. Every week of the coming season we shall send personal conductors with parties to Paris ; and every week, or alternate week, to Brussels, the Rhine, the Black Forest, Switzerland, the Italian Lakes, and round Italy. For ten travellers we furnish a conductor, and parties may be arranged by themselves without our intervention. In other cases public notice is given, and the arrangements are open to all who choose to avail themselves of them.

HOTEL ACCOMMODATION COUPONS

ORIGINATED AND ISSUED BY

THOMAS COOK AND SON.

The HOTEL COUPON business, which was commenced as a friendly arrangement of mutual interest to ourselves, to Hotel Proprietors, and Tourists, has far exceeded our most sanguine anticipations; and as its benefits become better known, they will be more highly appreciated by all who are interested in the success of the scheme.

The European Hotel Coupons are issued at the uniform rate of 8s. per day, and are arranged as follows:—1st Coupon (yellow).—*Breakfast*, specifying of what it shall consist. 2nd Coupon (red). —*Dinner at Table d'Hote*, with or without Wine, according to the custom of the Hotels. 3rd Coupon (blue).—*Bed-room*, including *lights* and *attendance*.

These are the ordinary features of Continental Hotel life, all else being regarded as extras, and as such they are left to be paid for by Supplemental Coupons or Cash.

The Coupons are accepted at full value at one principal Hotel in each of the chief cities, towns, and places of Tourist resort in Switzerland, Italy, on the banks of the Rhine, and a a great many places in France, Germany, Holland, Belgium, Austria, &c.; also for meals on board the Great Eastern Channel Steamers and the Rhine Steamers.

SUPPLEMENTAL AND EXCEPTIONAL ARRANGEMENTS.

In LONDON Tourists may be accommodated *en route* to or from the Continent at COOK's British Museum Boarding House, 59, Great Russell Street, Bloomsbury, at 6s. per day, for Bed, Breakfast, and Tea with meats. (Hotel Coupons accepted at their full value in payment).

Hotel Coupons are also accepted at the London and Paris Hotel and Refreshment Rooms, NEW-HAVEN WHARF. Coupons are accepted for meals on board the GREAT EASTERN CHANNEL STEAMERS, and on the RHINE STEAMERS.

SPECIAL COUPONS are issued for VIENNA, available at the Hotel de l'Union, and Hotel Metropole, at 13s. per day.

For PARIS, Hotel Coupons at special rates are issued for the Grand Hotel, and for the Hotel Bedford. In PARIS, the other Hotels in Messrs. COOK & SON's connection are not equal in appearance and style to those of the Continent generally; but the proprietors having long evinced a kindly interest in promoting the comfort and convenience of Excursionists and Tourists, the Coupons are allowed to be accepted at the London and New York Hotel, Place du Havre; Hotel St. Petersburg, 35, Rue Caumartin; at the Hotel Beretta (late Londres) 8, Rue St. Hyacinthe, Rue St. Honoré. For these Hotels, accommodation cards are also issued at the rate of 8s. per day, including meat for Breakfast. SPECIAL COUPONS are issued on the Grand Hotel, at 16s. per day, and on the Hotel Bedford at 12s. per day.

At ROUEN, Mrs. Daniells, widow of the late Interpreter at the Station, who keeps a small Hotel, the Victoria, near the Station, wishes to accept Coupons from parties breaking their journey there.

ADDITIONAL CHARGES are made on the Coupons as follows:—

AT BADEN-BADEN, at the time of the Races, 2 francs per day.

AT ROME, from the first of April to the end of April, from 1 franc to 3 francs per day, according to the class of rooms, are now agreed to as extra charges, but new arrangements may have to be made in consequence of Rome being now the capital of Italy. Whatever change is made, notice will be given thereof.

AT THE RIGI KULM Hotels, 1 franc extra is required on the bed-room Coupon: All these extras can be paid by Supplemental Coupons or Cash. Travellers wishing to spend the night at this Hotel must give at least one day's notice by letter or telegram to the Manager, stating that they hold "Cook's Coupons," and wish rooms reserved.

GIESSBACH.—The Dinner Coupons can only be accepted at this hotel when the passengers remain for the night.

CONDITIONS and terms of REPAYMENT for unused Coupons are printed in the Coupon Books.

ANY COMPLAINTS which parties have to make as to the use of the Coupons, or the conduct of Hotel Proprietors or Servants, to be addressed, in writing, to Messrs. THOMAS COOK & SON, Ludgate Circus, Fleet Street, London.

COUPONS CAN BE OBTAINED at the offices of Messrs. THOMAS COOK & SON, Ludgate Circus, and 445, West Strand, London; Cases Street (opposite New Central Station), Liverpool; 43, Piccadilly, Manchester; 16. Stephenson Place, New Street, Birmingham; 15, Place du Havre, Paris; 22, Galerie du Roi, Brussels; 40, Dombof, Cologne; 90, Rue du Rhône, Geneva; 1a, Piazza di Spagna, Rome; and also at the Hotels Swan, Lucerne; Trois Rois, Bâle; Trombetta, Turin; Victoria, Venice.

REPAYMENTS FOR UNUSED HOTEL COUPONS, less 10 per cent., can only be made at the Chief Office, Ludgate Circus, Fleet Street, London, and no agents are authorised to repay for any not used.

HOTELS IN THE EAST.—A special series of Coupons is provided for the East Levant, and we append List of Hotels.

FOR SCOTLAND AND IRELAND also a special series is provided, as per Programmes

EUROPEAN AND EASTERN HOTELS

Where Cook's Coupons for Hotel Accommodation will be accepted.

HOTELS IN FRANCE AND FRENCH SAVOY.

AIX LES BAINS—Hotel de la Paix.
AMIENS—Hotel de l'Univers.
AMPHION (Lake of Geneva)—Grand Hotel des [Bains.
ANNECY, Hotel d'Angleterre.
BAGNERES DE BIOORRE—Hotel de France.
BORDEAUX—Hotel de France.
BOULOGNE—Grand Hotel Christol.
CALAIS—Hotel Dessin.
CANNES—Hotel Beau Site.
CHAMBERY—Hotel de la Poste. [Royal.
CHAMOUNY—Hotel de l'Angleterre, and Hotel
DIEPPE—Hotel Queen Victoria.
DIJON—Hotel Jura.
FONTAINEBLEAU—Hotel de Londres.
GORGES DU FIER—Châlet Hotel.
GRENOBLE—Hotel Monnet.
HYERES—Hotel des Iles d'Or.
LYONS—Hotel de l'Europe.

MACON—Hotel de l'Europe.
MARSEILLES—Hotel du Louvre et de la Pa
MENTONE—Hotel Grande Bretagne.
MODANE— { Grand Hotel International.
{ Station Buffet.
NICE—Grand Hotel.
PONTARLIER—Hotel de la Poste.
*PARIS— ⎰ Grand Hotel (Special Coupons).
⎟ Bedford Hotel (Special Coupons).
⎨ Londres et New York, Place du Havre.
⎟ St. Petersbourg, 35, rue Caumartin.
⎱ Londres, 8, rue St. Hyacinthe
* See special note on cover of Hotel Coupon
PAU—Grand Hotel Gassion.
ROUEN—Smith's Albion Hotel.
SEMNOZ ALPS—Chalet Hotel de Semnoz.
TOULON—Grand Hotel.
VICHY—Grand Hotel des Bains.

ALGERIA AND TUNIS.

ALGIERS—
BATNA—Hotel de Paris.
BISKRA—Hotel du Sahara.
BLIDAH—Hotel d'Orient.
BONA—Hotel d'Orient.
CONSTANTINE—Hotel d'Orient.

GUELMA—Hotel Auriel.
ORAN—Hotel de la Paix.
TLEMCEN—Hotel de France.
TUNIS—Hotel de Paris.
SOUKAHRAS—Hotel Thagaste.

HOTELS IN SICILY.

CATANIA—Grand Hotel.
MESSINA—Hotel Victoria.
PALERMO—Hotel de France.

SYRACUSE—Hotel Victoria.
TAORMINA—Hotel Timeo.

SWITZERLAND AND THE ALPINE DISTRICTS.

AARAU—Hotel de la Cigogne.
AIGLE—Hotel Victoria.
AIROLO—Hotel de la Poste.
ALPNACHT—Hotel Pilatus.
ANDERMATT—Hotel Trois Rois.
BADEN (Switzerland)—Hinterhof.
BALE—Hotel Trois Rois.
BERNE—Hotel Belle Vue. [Ville.
BELLINZONA—Hotel de l'Ange, and Hotel de la
BEX—Hotel des Bains.
BIASCA—Hotel de Biasca.
BRIENZ—Hotel de la Croix Blanche.
BRIGUE—Hotel de la Poste.
CHAUX DE FONDS—Hotel de la Fleur de Lis.
COIRE—Hotel Steinbock.
EINSIEDELN—Hotel du Paon.
ENGELBERG—Hotel Sonnenberg.
FALLS of the RHINE (Neuhausen)—Schweizerhof
FLUELEN— Hotel Croix Blanche et Poste.
FRIBOURG—Hotel Zæheringen.
GENEVA— { Grand Hotel de Russie et Anglo-
{ Hotel du Lac. [Americain.
GIESSBACH. Hotel Giessbach.
GRINDELWALD—Hotel de l'Aigle Noir.
HOSPENTHAL—Meyerhof.
INTERLACKEN— { Hotel Victoria.
{ Hotel Ritchard.
LA TOUR—Hotel du Rivage.
LAUSANNE— { Hotel Gibbon.
{ Hotel d'Angleterre, Ouchy.
LAUTERBRUNNEN—Hotel du Capricorne.
LEUKERBAD—Hotels des Alps and Belle Vue.

LOCLE—Hotel Jura.
LUCERNE—Hotel du Cygne (Swan).
LUNGERN— { Hotel du Lion d'Or.
{ Hotel Oberwald.
LUGANO—Hotel du Parc and Station Buffet.
MARTIGNY—Hotel Clerc.
MEIRINGEN—Hotel du Sauvage.
MENDRISIO—Hotel Mendrisio.
MONTE GENEROSO—Hotel de Monteroso. [Lac.
MONTREUX—Langbein's Hotel Beau-Séjour au
MORGES—Hotel des Alpes.
NEUCHATEL—Grand Hotel du Lac.
RAGATZ—Hotel Quellenhof.
RIGI-KULM— { Hotel du Rigi-Kulm.
{ Hotel Schreiber.
RIGI-STAFFEL—Hotel Rigi-Staffel.
RORSCHACH—Hotel Sechof.
ROVIO—Hotel Rovio.
SAMADEN—Hotel Bernina.
SARNEN— { Brunig Hotel.
{ Hotel de l'Oberwald.
ST. GALL—Hotel de St. Gall.
ST. NICHOLAS—Grand Hotel.
SIERRE—Hotel Belle Vue.
SPLUGEN—Hotel de la Poste.
THOUNE (Thun)— { Hotel Belle Vue
{ Grand Hotel de Thoune.
THUSIS—Hotel Via Mala.
TRIENT—Hotel du Glacier de Trient.
VEVEY—Grand Hotel Vevey.
VERNAYAZ—Hotel des Gorges de Trient.
ZURICH—Hotel Belle Vue.

HOTELS IN BLACK FOREST.

ALBBRUCK- Hotel Albthal.
BRENNET (Station)—Hotel Werrathal.
BELCHEN (High Mountain Station)—Rasthaus Belchen.
DONAUESCHINGEN—Hotel Schutzen.
FELDBERG (High Mountain Station)—Hotel Feldbergerhof.
FURTWANGEN—Angel Hotel.
GERNSBACH—Bath Hotel.
HOCHEN SCHWAND—Hotel Maler.
HOLSTEIG (Hollenthal)—Golden Star Hotel.
HORNBERG—Hotel Baren.
LORRACH—Hirsch Hotel.
LENZKIRCH—Hotel Poste.
MULHEIM—Hotel Kittler.
NEUSTADT—Hotel Poste.
OTTENHOFEN—Hotel Pflug.

OBERKIRCH—Hotel Linde.
SCHLUCHSEE—Hotel Star.
SACKINGEN—Hotel Schutzen.
SCHONAU—Hotel Sonne.
SCHOPFHEIM—Hotel Three Kings.
ST. GEORGEN (Black Forest)—Hotel Hirsch.
ST. BLASIEN—Hotel St. Blasien.
TODTNAU—Hotel Ochsen.
TRIBERG (Town)—Lion Hotel.
TRIBERG (Cascade)—Black Forest Hotel.
VOHRENBACH—Hotel Kreuz.
VILLENGEN—Hotel Blume (Poste).
WALDKIRCH—Hotel Poste.
WALDSHUT—Hotel Kulmer.
WALFACH—Hotel Krone.
WEHR (Werrathal)—Hotel Krone.

BELGIUM, HOLLAND, THE RHINE, GERMANY, AND AUSTRIA.

ADELSBERG—Grand Hotel.
AIX-LA-CHAPELLE—Hotel du Dragon d'Or.
AMSTERDAM—Old Bible Hotel.
ANTWERP—{ Hotel de la Paix. Hotel de l'Europe.
AUGSBURG—Hotel de Baviere.
BADEN-BADEN—Hotel de Hollande.
BERLIN—{ Markgraft's Hotel de l'Europe. Hotel Bartickow. Töpfer's Hotel.
BINGEN—Hotel Victoria.
BONN—Grand Hotel Royal.
BOPPARD—Hotel du Rhin.
BOTZEN- Hotel Kaiserkrone (Imperial Crown).
BREDA—Hotel Swan.
BREMEN—Hotel de l'Europe.
BRIXEN—Elephant Hotel.
BRUGES—Hotel de Flandre.
BRUSSELS—{ Hotel de la Poste. Hotel du Grand Miroir.
CARLSRUHE—Hotel zum Erbprinz.
COBLENCE—Hotel du Geant.
COLOGNE—Hotels Belle Vue and Hollande.
CONSTANCE—Hotel Hecht.
DARMSTADT—Hotel Traube.
DRESDEN—Grand Union Hotel.
EMS—Hotel Darmstadt.
FIELD OF WATERLOO—Museum Hotel.
FRANKFORT - Grand Hotel du Nord.
FREIBURG (Baden)-Hotel Trescher zum Pfaum.

GHENT—Hotel de Vienne.
HAMBURG—Hotel Strcit.
HANOVER—British Hotel.
HEIDELBERG—Hotel de l'Europe.
INNSBRUCK—Hotel Tyrol.
KIEL—Hotel Germania.
MAYENCE—Hotel de Hollande.
METZ—{ Hotel de Paris. Grand Hotel de Metz.
MUNICH—Hotel Belle Vue.
NAMUR—Hotel Holland.
NEUWIED—Moravian Hotel.
OSTEND—Hotel d'Allemagne.
PASSAU—Hotel Bayrischen Hof.
REGENSBURG—Hotel Three Helmets.
RENDSBURG—Hotel Bergmau.
ROCHEFORT—Hotel Biron.
ROTTERDAM—New Bath Hotel.
SALZBURG—Hotel Erzherzog Carl.
SCHWALBACH—Hotel Metropole.
SPA—Hotel de l'Europe.
STETTIN—Hotel du Nord.
STRASBURG—Hotel Maison Rouge.
STUTTGARDT—Marquardt's Hotel.
THE HAGUE—Hotel du Vieux Doelen.
TRIESTE—Hotel de la Ville.
VIENNA—{ Special Union Hotel. Hotel Coupons Hotel Metropole.
WIESBADEN—Grand Hotel du Rhin.
WORMS—Hotel de l'Europe.

SWEDEN, NORWAY, AND DENMARK.

AARHUUS—Hotel Royal.
CHRISTIANIA—Grand Hotel.
COPENHAGEN—Hotel d'Angleterre.
HELSINGBORG—Hotel Molberg.

HONEFOS—Gladvett's Hotel.
JONKOPING—Hotel Jonkoping.
STOCKHOLM—{ Grand Hotel. Hotel Rydberg.

HOTELS IN ITALY.

ALASSIO- Hotel de Londres.
ANCONA—Hotel della Pace.
ARONA—Hotel de l'Italie.
BELLAGIO—Hotel Grande Bretagne.
BOLOGNA—Hotel Brun.
BORDIGHERA—Hotel d'Angleterre.
BRINDISI—Hotel Oriental.
CADENABBIA (Lake of Como)- Grand Hotel Belle Vue.
CAPRI—Hotel du Louvre.
CASERTA—Hotel Victoria.
CASTELLAMARE—Hotel Royal.
CERNOBBIO (Lake of Como)- Grand Hotel Villa d'Este.
COMO (ON LAKE)—Hotel de la Reine d'Angleterre.
CORFU (Greece)—Hotel St. George.
CORNIGLIANO—Grand Hotel Villa Rachel.
CHIAVENNA—Hotel Conradi.
CHIASSO—Hotel Chiasso.
DOMO D'OSSOLA—Hotel de la Ville.
FLORENCE—{ Hotel New York. Hotel de l'Europo. English & American Boarding House Palazzo d'Elci, 28, via Maggio.
GENOA—Hotels de la Ville and Trombetta Feder.
ISCHIA (Casamicciola)—Hotel Belle Vue.
LA TOUR—Hotel de l'Ours.

LEGHORN—Hotel Du Nord.
LUCCA—Hotel de l'Univers.
MANTUA—Hotel de l'Ecu de France.
MENAGGIO—Hotel Victoria.
MILAN—{ Hotel Royal. Station Buffet.
NAPLES—Hotel des Etrangers.
PADUA—Hotel Stella d'Oro.
PALLANZA—Grand Hotel l'allanza.
PARMA—
PERUGIA—Hotel de Perugia.
PISA—Hotel de Londres.
POMPEII—Hotel Diomede.
ROME—Hotel d'Allemagne.
SALERNO—Hotel Victoria.
SAN REMO—Hotel Victoria.
SIENNA—Grand Hotel.
SONDRIO (Valtelina)—Hotel de la Poste.
SORRENTO—Hotel Tramontano.
SPEZIA—Hotel de la Croix de Malte.
STRESA—Hotel des Isles Borromees.
SYRACUSE—Hotel Victoria.
†TURIN—Hotel Trombetta.
VARESE—Grand Hotel Varese.
†VENICE—Hotel Victoria.
VERONA—{ Hotel Tower of London. Station Buffet.

At the Hotels marked thus † Cook's Tickets may be had.

EASTERN HOTELS (SPECIAL COUPONS).

ALEXANDRIA— Hotel de l'Europe.
CAIRO—Shepheard's Hotel and the New Hotel.
SUEZ—Suez Hotel.
PORT SAID—Hotel de France & Hotel du Louvre.
JERUSALEM — { Mediterranean Hotel.
{ Hotel de l'Europe.
JAFFA—Twelve Tribes Hotel (Cook's Agency).
BEYROUT—Hotel Bellevue.
DAMASCUS -Dimetris Hotel.
CONSTANTINOPLE—Hotel de Luxemburg.
ATHENS—Hotel des Etrangers.

HOTELS IN ENGLAND, IRELAND, AND SCOTLAND.

ENGLAND.

ASHBURTON—Golden Lion Hotel.
BIDEFORD—Tantou's Hotel.
 ,, —New Inn.
BARNSTAPLE—Royal and Fortescue Hotels.
 ,, —Golden Lion Hotel.
BUDE—Falcon Hotel.
DARTMOUTH—Castle Hotel.
 ,, —Royal Dart Yacht Club Hotel, Kingswear.
EXETER- Royal Clarence Hotel.
 ,, —New London Hotel
FALMOUTH –Falmouth Hotel.
ILFRACOMBE—Royal Clarence Hotel.
 ,, —Ilfracombe Hotel.

KINGSBRIDGE—King's Arms Hotel.
LAUNCESTON—White Hart Hotel.
MINEHEAD—Feathers Hotel.
NEWTON ABBOT—Globe Hotel.
PENZANCE—Queen's Hotel.
 ,, —Lavin's Mount's Bay Hotel.
 ,, —Union Hotel.
SLAPTON SANDS—Tor Cross Hotel.
TAUNTON—Railway Hotel.
TAVISTOCK—Queen's Hotel.
TOTNES—Seymour Hotel.
TORQUAY—Royal Hotel.
WESTWARD HO—Royal Hotel.

IRELAND.

BELFAST—Queen's Hotel.
BUNDORAN—Hamilton's Hotel.
CORK—Imperial Hotel.
 ,, —Victoria Hotel.
COLERAINE—Clothworkers' Arms Hotel.
DUBLIN—Morrison's Hotel.
 ,, —Imperial.
ENNISKILLEN—Royal Hotel.
GALWAY—Railway Hotel.
GLENGARRIFF—Roche's Hotel.
 ,, —Eccles' Hotel.
INCHIGEELA—Lake Hotel.

KILLARNEY—Victoria Hotel.
 ,, —Railway Hotel.
KENMARE -Lansdowne Arms Hotel.
LIMERICK—Royal Hotel.
LONDONDERRY—Jury's Hotel.
PORTRUSH—Antrim Arms Hotel.
QUEENSTOWN—Queen's Hotel.
RATHNEW, co. Wicklow–Newrath Bridge Hotel.
SLIGO—Imperial Hotel.
STRABANE—Abercorn Arms Hotel
WATERFORD—Imperial Hotel.
WESTPORT—Mrs. Gilder's Hotel.

SCOTLAND.

ABERDEEN—Forsyth's Hotel.
BANAVIE—The Lochiel Arms.
BALLACHULISH—Ballachulish Hotel.
DUNKELD—Royal Hotel.
 ,, Athole Arms Hotel.
EDINBURGH—Philp's Cockburn Hotel.
GLASGOW—Forsyth's Cobden Hotel.
 ,, —Washington Hotel.

INVERNESS—Waverley Hotel.
MELROSE—George Hotel.
OBAN—Caledonian Hotel.
PERTH—Pople's British Hotel.
PITLOCHRIE—Fisher's Royal Hotel.
PORTREE, Isle of Skye—Royal Hotel.
STIRLING—Golden Lion Hotel.

THOMAS COOK AND SON, TOURIST OFFICES, LUDGATE CIRCUS, LONDON.

BRANCH OFFICES.

Cook's West-end Agency, 445, West Strand, opposite Charing Cross Station and Hotel.

BIRMINGHAM—16, Stephenson Place.
MANCHESTER—43, Piccadilly.
LIVERPOOL—14, Cases Street.
LEEDS—1, Royal Exchange.
BRADFORD—In Front of Midland Station.
DUBLIN—45, Dame Street.
EDINBURGH—9, Princes Street.
PARIS—15, Place du Havre.

COLOGNE—40, Domhof.
BRUSSELS—22, Galerie du Roi.
GENEVA—-90, Rue du Rhone.
ROME—1b, Piazza di Spagna.
CAIRO—Cook's Tourist Pavilion, Shepheard's Hotel.
JAFFA—Twelve Tribes Hotel.

American House—Cook, Son & Jenkins, 261, Broadway, New York.

OFFICES AND AGENCIES
OF
THOMAS COOK AND SON.

CHIEF OFFICE :—Ludgate Circus, Fleet Street, London.

BRANCH OFFICES:

LONDON { West-end Agency—445, West Strand; and
Corner of Midland Station, St. Pancras.

BIRMINGHAM—16, Stephenson Place.
MANCHESTER—43, Piccadilly.
LIVERPOOL—14, Cases Street.
LEEDS—1, Royal Exchange.

BRADFORD—In Front of Midland Station.
LEICESTER—63, Granby Street.
DUBLIN—45, Dame Street.
EDINBURGH—9, Princes Street.

CONTINENTAL OFFICES:

PARIS—15, Place du Havre.
BRUSSELS—22, Galerie du Roi.
COLOGNE—40, Domhof.

GENEVA—90, Rue du Rhône.
ROME—1D, Piazza di Spagna.

AGENCIES:

Bristol—Mr. MACK, 38, Park Street.
Exeter—R. P. CULLEY & Co., 226, High Street.
Sheffield — Mr. RODGERS, Change Alley Corner.
Newcastle-on-Tyne—Mr. FRANKLIN, Bookseller, Mosley Street.
Edinburgh—Mr. PHILP, Cockburn Hotel.

Glasgow — Midland Office, 165, Buchanan Street.
Glasgow — Mr. FORSYTH, Cobden Hotel.
Cork—Mr. MURRAY, 90, George Street.
Belfast—Mr. GREER, Donegall Place.
Dundalk—Mr. C. P. COOPER.
Turin—Hotel Trombetta.
Venice—Hotel Victoria.

AGENCIES IN SWITZERLAND
(For the Sale of Hotel Coupons only):

Bale—Messrs. DE SPEYR & Co.
„ Hotel Trois Rois.
Lucerne—Hotel du Cygne.
Berne—Hotel Belle Vue.

Neuchatel—Hotel du Lac.
Martigny—Hotel Clerc.
Zurich—Hotel Bellevue.

CHIEF ORIENTAL OFFICES:
Cairo, Egypt—COOK'S Pavilion, Shepheard's Hotel.
Jaffa, Palestine—COOK'S Agency, Twelve Tribes Hotel.
Alexandria—Hotel de l'Europe.

AMERICAN OFFICES:
COOK, SON & JENKINS,
WORLD'S TICKET OFFICE, CENTENNIAL EXHIBITION, PHILADELPHIA.

New York—261, Broadway.
Boston—104, Washington Street.
Washington—701, Fifteenth Street (opposite Treasury Department).
Philadelphia—614, Chestnut Street.

New Orleans—29, Carondelet Street.
New Haven—74, Church Street.
San Francisco — 3, New Montgomery Street.

EASTERN DRAGOMAN CONTRACTOR AND DIRECTOR:
Mr. ALEXANDER HOWARD, of Beyrout and Jaffa.

MIDLAND RAILWAY.

PULLMAN CAR TRAINS
BETWEEN
LIVERPOOL AND LONDON,
AND
LONDON AND MANCHESTER, LEEDS, AND BRADFORD.

The Midland Railway Company are now running a Train of the celebrated American Pullman Drawing-room and Sleeping Cars between London and Liverpool, and between London and Manchester, Leeds and Bradford, in each direction daily, Sundays excepted.

These Trains convey First and Third Class Passengers at Ordinary Fares in Midland Pullman Cars, and First Class Passengers may avail themselves of the American Pullman Drawing-room and Sleeping Cars at a small additional charge.

A Train of Midland Pullman Cars runs between Manchester and Marple, in connection with the Up and Down Trains to and from Liverpool.

A Train of American Pullman Sleeping Cars leaves the St. Pancras Station, London, at 12·0 midnight (Sundays excepted), for Manchester, Liverpool, Sheffield, Leeds, and Bradford. Passengers for Manchester, availing themselves of the Sleeping Car, have to change at Marple.

The Night Train is placed ready for departure from London at ten o'clock, and Passengers may enter their berths at any time that suits their convenience after that hour.

The Midland Company are now running a Special Service of Express and Fast Trains between LIVERPOOL and LONDON, with their own Engines and Carriages. These Trains run through the most picturesque portion of the celebrated Peak of Derbyshire, and the Vale of Matlock.

The Midland Company's Trains arrive at and depart from the St. Pancras Station, London, and the Central Station, Ranelagh Street, Liverpool.

The Midland Grand Hotel (one of the largest Hotels in Europe), containing upwards of 400 Bed-rooms, with spacious Coffee-room, Reading-room, and numerous Drawing-rooms, has been erected by the Company at the St. Pancras Terminus, and will be found replete with every accommodation.

BRIGHTON.—A Pullman Drawing-room Car Train runs every week day between Victoria and Brighton, leaving Victoria at 10·45 a.m., returning from Brighton at 5·45 p.m.

Berths, Seats, and Saloons for Pullman Cars can be secured by applying in advance at any of the offices of

THOS. COOK AND SON,
Chief Office, Ludgate Circus, London.

COOK'S
EXCURSIONS, TOURS,
AND
GENERAL TRAVELLING ARRANGEMENTS.

THOMAS COOK AND SON,

Pioneers, Inaugurators, and Promoters of the principal systems of Tours established in Great Britain and Ireland, and on the Continent of Europe, are now giving increased attention to Ordinary Travelling Arrangements, with a view to rendering them as easy, practicable, and economical as circumstances will allow. During 35 years more than FOUR MILLIONS of Travellers have visited near and distant places under their arrangements; and their system of Tickets now provides for visiting the chief points of interest in the Four Quarters of the Globe.

Cook's West of England Tours, combining Railway, Coach, and Steamer to every point of interest between Bristol and the Land's End. The Tickets are prepared in Coupon form, and can be issued in combination, to meet the requirements of the Tourist. Hotel Coupons are also issued for First Class Hotels in the District.

Cook's Scotch Tours cover all points of Tourist interest in Scotland, Oban, Staffa, Iona, Isle of Skye, Caledonian Canal, Kyles of Bute, the Trossachs, the Highlands, the Lake District, Edinburgh, &c.; and can be used in a similar manner to the Irish Tours.

Cook's Irish Tours.—THOMAS COOK & SON issue Tourist Tickets to and through all parts of Ireland, including the Giant's Causeway, Belfast, Dublin, Galway, Loch Erne, the Lakes of Killarney, &c. They can be used in connection with Tickets from London, or any town on the Midland Railway.

Cook's Tickets to Paris are available by the Shortest and Cheapest Routes, and by Dover and Calais.

Cook's Swiss Tickets are available by every Route, and cover every part of the country. **Thomas Cook & Son** are the only Authorized Agents of every Swiss Railway, Steamboat, and Diligence Company. Every Alpine Route is included in their arrangements.

Cook's Italian Tickets provide for every Route to and through Italy, and are offered at great Reductions in Fares.

Cook's Tours to Holland, Belgium, and the Rhine, are arranged upon a most comprehensive basis, Tickets being provided for every Route, for single and return journeys, and for Circular Tours. Breaks of journey are allowed at all places of interest.

Cook's Personally-conducted Tours have become a most popular feature in their arrangements. Parties are organized to leave London weekly during the season for Switzerland, Germany, Italy, and various parts of the Continent.

The Steam Navigation of the Nile is committed by the Khédive Government entirely to **Thomas Cook & Son**. The Steamers (the only ones on the Nile) ply between Cairo and the First Cataract (600 miles), and the Second Cataract (810 miles). Tickets can be had, and berths secured, at any of **Thomas Cook & Son's Offices.**

Tours to Palestine are rendered easy, safe, and economical, by the superior arrangements of **Thomas Cook & Son**, who now have their own Resident Manager in Beyrout and Jaffa. They are therefore prepared to conduct large or small parties in the most comfortable manner through the country; to Jerusalem, the Dead Sea, the Jordan, Damascus, Sinai, &c. The parties can be so fixed as to go independently or under personal management any time between October and April. Over nine hundred ladies and gentlemen have visited Palestine under their arrangements.

Turkey, Greece, the Levant, &c.—Thomas Cook & Son are now prepared to issue Tickets by any line of Steamers, to any port touched by the Austrian Lloyd's, Messageries Maritimes, and Rubattino Co.'s Steamers.

India, China, &c.—Thomas Cook & Son are the Agents of the principal Steamship Companies of the world, and are prepared to issue Tickets from Southampton, Venice, Ancona, Genoa, Naples, and Brindisi, to Alexandria, Aden, Bombay, Calcutta, Singapore, Hong Kong, Shanghai, or any other point in India or China.

Algerian Tours.—Messrs. Thomas Cook & Son issue Tickets by any route to Algeria, and over the Algerian Railways and Diligences.

Round the World.—Thomas Cook & Son are prepared to issue a direct travelling Ticket for a journey Round the World by Steam, available to go either West or East. First Class, from £190.

Cook's Hotel Coupons, available at over three hundred first-class hotels in various parts of the world, can be had by travellers purchasing **Cook's Tourist Tickets**, guaranteeing them first class accommodations at fixed and regular prices.

Passages to America and Canada are secured by **Thomas Cook & Son** for all the chief lines of Steamers. Arrangements are made for Tours through America, giving a choice of more than 200 Single and Tourist Tickets; and an Office has been opened in New York, under the joint arrangement of **Cook, Son and Jenkins**, 261, Broadway.

Thomas Cook & Son's General Travelling Arrangements are so widely extended that they can supply Tickets to almost any point that Tourists may wish to visit, in many cases at reductions, many ranging from twenty-five to forty-five per cent. below ordinary fares. The regular Travelling Ticket being issued in all cases, printed in English on one side, and in the language of the country where it is used on the other, and it contains all the information the traveller needs.

Policies of Insurance against accidents of all kinds, by land and sea, are effected through the Office of Messrs. Cook & Son, as Agents of the "Ocean, Railway, and General Accident Assurance Company, Limited."

Programmes can be had gratuitously, on application at the Offices of Thomas Cook & Son, or by post, in return for stamps covering postage.

Cook's Excursionist is published at short intervals during the season in London, New York, and Brussels, at 2d., post free, 3d., and contains programmes and lists to the number of nearly one thousand specimen Tours, Tickets for which are issued by **Thomas Cook & Son**, with fares by every route.

Cook's Continental Time Tables and Tourist Handbook, with Eight Sectional Maps, price 1s., post free.

THOMAS COOK & SON,
CHIEF OFFICE:
LUDGATE CIRCUS, FLEET STREET, LONDON, E.C.
WEST-END AGENCY:
445, West Strand (opposite Charing Cross Station and Hotel).

INTERESTING WORK FOR TRAVELLERS.

Handsomely bound in cloth gilt, Vols. I. and II., price 4s. 6d. each.

ALL THE WORLD OVER:
A WORK OF TRAVEL, INCIDENT, LEGEND, AND RESEARCH.
Edited by EDWIN HODDER, F.R.G.S.

Embellished with Handsome Maps, and Profusely Illustrated.

LIST OF MAPS.

Vol. I.	Vol. II.
ALGERIA.	PLAN OF POMPEII.
NAPLES and ENVIRONS.	PLAN OF VENICE.
GREECE.	MAP of EASTERN TOURS.
SWITZERLAND.	,, EGYPT.
SWEDEN and NORWAY.	,, HOLLAND AND BELGIUM.
PANORAMA of the RHINE.	,, ITALY.

THE FIRST VOLUME CONTAINS

Birds of Passage; or, A Six Weeks' Romance (complete in Nineteen Chapters). By T. AMBROSE HEATH.

ARTICLES on Algeria, Norway, Sweden, The Far North, Ceylon, Italian Lakes, Naples and Thereabouts, Lake of Geneva, The Ardennes; Our Travellers' Club, &c., &c.

THE SECOND VOLUME CONTAINS

A Love Chase; or, Autumn Manœuvres (complete in Twelve Chapters). By T. AMBROSE HEATH.

On the Track of the Pilgrim Fathers; A Ride through the Sabines; Field Sports in Ceylon; Our Holiday in Sweden; Alexandria and Cairo, The North Cape, Ragusa, Venice, Mount Etna, Mont St. Michel, City of Goa, The Jumping Procession at Echternach, The Judengasse at Frankfort-on-the-Main, Lake of Zurich, Winter Residence in Torquay, Travel Talk, Our Travellers' Club, &c., &c.

And a variety of interesting matter contributed by well-known Authors and Travellers.

THOS. COOK & SON, LUDGATE CIRCUS, LONDON;

Sold also by COOK, SON & JENKINS, at the WORLD'S TICKET OFFICE, Centennial Exhibition, Philadelphia.

www.ingramcontent.com/pod-product-compliance
Lightning Source LLC
Chambersburg PA
CBHW022151090426
42742CB00010B/1470